SELECTED
WILLIAM WO

from Kathryn:
Windermere, June 1973

THE POETRY BOOKSHELF

General Editor: James Reeves

Robert Graves: *English and Scottish Ballads*
Tom Scott: *Late Medieval Scots Poetry*
James Reeves: *Chaucer: Lyric and Allegory*
William Tydeman: *English Poetry 1400–1580*
Martin Seymour-Smith: *Shakespeare's Sonnets*
Martin Seymour-Smith: *Longer Elizabethan Poems*
James Reeves: *John Donne*
Maurice Hussey: *Jonson and the Cavaliers*
Jack Dalglish: *Eight Metaphysical Poets*
James Reeves and Martin Seymour-Smith: *Andrew Marvell*
Gareth Reeves: *George Herbert*
Dennis Burden: *Shorter Poems of John Milton*
V. de S. Pinto: *Poetry of the Restoration*
Roger Sharrock: *John Dryden*
James Reeves: *Jonathan Swift*
John Heath-Stubbs: *Alexander Pope*
Francis Venables: *The Early Augustans*
Donald Davie: *The Late Augustans*
F. W. Bateson: *William Blake*
G. S. Fraser: *Robert Burns*
Roger Sharrock: *William Wordsworth*
James Reeves: *S. T. Coleridge*
Robin Skelton: *Lord Byron*
John Holloway: *P. B. Shelley*
James Reeves: *John Clare*
Robert Gittings: *Poems and Letters of John Keats*
Edmund Blunden: *Alfred Lord Tennyson*
James Reeves: *Robert Browning*
Denys Thompson: *Poetry and Prose of Matthew Arnold*
James Reeves: *Emily Dickinson*
James Reeves: *G. M. Hopkins*
David Wright: *Seven Victorian Poets*
James Reeves: *The Modern Poets' World*
James Reeves: *D. H. Lawrence*

SELECTED POEMS OF

WILLIAM WORDSWORTH

*Edited with an Introduction
and Notes
by*

ROGER SHARROCK

HEINEMANN
LONDON

Heinemann Educational Books Ltd

LONDON EDINBURGH MELBOURNE AUCKLAND TORONTO
SINGAPORE HONG KONG KUALA LUMPUR
IBADAN NAIROBI JOHANNESBURG
NEW DELHI

ISBN 0 435 15014 6 (cased edition)
ISBN 0 435 15015 4 (paperback)

WILLIAM WORDSWORTH 1770–1850

Published by
Heinemann Educational Books Ltd
48 Charles Street, London W1X 8AH
Printed in Great Britain by Morrison and Gibb Ltd
London and Edinburgh

CONTENTS

INTRODUCTION

1. WORDSWORTH IN OUR TIME

WORDSWORTH'S greatness is secure, but in the century since his death the nature of his reputation has shifted and changed more than is usual with that of a major poet. He himself was aware that he would have to form the taste by which he would be enjoyed, and he educated his public slowly and painfully without concessions to their stock responses or to the ordinary social delights of literature. The handful of readers whose imaginative world had been altered by the impact of *Lyrical Ballads* grew gradually into a Wordsworthian public. In the hands of the Edinburgh Reviewers his name was a symbol of literary anarchism and wilful absurdity; as De Quincey says, it became militant between 1820 and 1830, and after 1830 triumphant.

The Victorians revered him as the apostle of the consolation of nature; in Arnold's words

> He laid us as we were at birth
> On the cool, flowery lap of earth.

They went to Grasmere by the railway which Wordsworth had abhorred and resisted; they looked at landscape through the new eyes he had given them and found a solace for urban man perplexed by the upheavals of faith and society in the world of Tennyson's despair and Arnold's ironic melancholy. Their admiration was chiefly for the sublime and spiritualizing in Wordsworth, the great *Ode* and *Tintern Abbey*, and the lyrical poems of delicate and minute observation on birds and flowers. They did not try to crack the nut on which the Edinburgh

Reviewers had broken their teeth, the defiant bathos of the early poetry; and, a deficiency for which they cannot be blamed but which coloured their whole outlook, they did not know the original version of *The Prelude* as Wordsworth read it to Coleridge in 1807. Their knowledge of his spiritual autobiography was gained from the text of 1850 in which so much had been altered, muffled, or suppressed in the revisions of his later years.

For in the course of his eighty years Wordsworth grew up as a man of the eighteenth century, survived the stresses of the romantic age, and finally assumed a hard outer crust of Victorianism; it was perhaps as good a protective covering as any for a great man against his admirers. Both the importance of his early partisanship of the French Revolution and his love affair with Annette Vallon, who bore him a daughter, were suppressed in the official biography by the poet's nephew, Christopher Wordsworth. The influential selection from the poems made by Matthew Arnold in 1879 set the seal on the nineteenth-century image of Wordsworth as a specialist in therapy and consolation working largely through the short lyric ; Arnold's anthology was also intended to save Wordsworth from becoming a cult in the hands of uncritical adherents of his philosophy of nature; it was well to ridicule the attempt to deduce a system from the poetry, a weakness of the age which found an opportunity for similar indulgence in Browning's works in the 'sixties and 'seventies. But like others who have tried to claim Wordsworth for the general reader Arnold refused to sympathize with a whole range of the poet's serious intentions and thus caused the appeal of much of the poetry to seem trivial.

However in this period he became at once the supreme poet for unpoetical people and an irresistible lure for the professional scholar. Men of affairs, stale with routine, sought and found consolation in his poetry; he spoke to the sensitive and intelligent without a literary training, like John Stuart Mill who, worn to the edge of breakdown by the aridly intellectual education his father had imposed on him, found in the poetry a 'culture of the feelings' which restored his spirit. The scholar on the other hand was attracted by the occurrence in Wordsworth of so many fundamental problems of the literary activity. The relation between poetry and doctrine, between language and experience, between autobiography and literature, is illuminated by Wordsworth's uncompromising reliance on his own insights, his refusal to make concessions to the social demands usually accepted by poetry.

The first quarter of the twentieth century saw a reorientation of our view of Wordsworth assisted by the work of scholarship. The biography by George McLean Harper (*William Wordsworth, His Life, Works and Influence*, 1916) was a landmark; so was the edition by Ernest de Selincourt of the 1805 text of *The Prelude* (published in 1926). The revolutionary Wordsworth with his republican passion and clandestine love affair was now brought into the light. Consideration of the young, liberal Wordsworth with his naturalistic creed of uninhibited joy encouraged the inquiry into the reason why this figure had been transformed into the Victorian 'Daddy Wordsworth', the author of the *Ecclesiastical Sonnets* and the butt of Max Beerbohm's cartoon which shows him prosing away in the rain to a bewildered little girl. The hypothesis of some major flaw of personality or of some psychological shock caused by the Annette affair became popular with biographers in an age of debunking, and was eloquently sustained by Sir Herbert Read (*Wordsworth*, 1930). Within the last twenty years a still further turn to the reputation of Wordsworth has been given by the great Oxford edition of Ernest de Selincourt and Helen Darbishire with its numerous variant readings based on original manuscripts, and by the former's edition of the letters. Now that such full materials for study are available it has been possible to turn back from biographical speculation to the poetry. There has after all, in the books written about Wordsworth since Coleridge's *Biographia Literaria*, been little enough on the poetry as poetry, too much piety or diversion into the philosophy of nature and politics. A number of appreciative critical studies have appeared recently which, though divergent in viewpoint, have this in common: a recognition that Wordsworth must be approached as a poet, seeking, however serious his matter, to move us by his use of language, not as a prophet or a psychological problem. Some, but by no means all of these critics believe that an artistic disaster, for which different reasons are assigned, overtook him in the middle of his career and impoverished his later poetry. But they are all agreed upon the normative value of a certain body of his work which is usually taken to be that written between his twenty-seventh and thirty-sixth years. Their books are read and discussed, and one gets the impression that the interest of a new generation in Wordsworth is keen and not inhibited by that rather laboured tendency to be found in older people whose literary education was exigent of a hard gem-like flame to laugh at the prosaic and moralizing element. Particularly interesting is the way in which *The Prelude* has come into its own; it can now be read for what it is a confessional vision of a single human life through the medium of intro-spection, and through this a window on human life in general, like Rousseau or Proust; it is no longer likely to be misunder-stood as an introduction to a system of thought—the title did a lot of harm.

It is the object of these selections to present Wordsworth to the general reader as a poet first and foremost, and in doing so to strike a balance between the different parts of his work. I have tried to represent both the shorter and the longer poems; the extracts from *The Prelude* are given in the version of 1805. It seemed best that *The Prelude* extracts—the story of the poet's mind—should introduce the rest, though they were written later than most of the *Lyrical Ballads*. The rest of the poems have been

arranged chronologically so far as that is possible. The selection
has not been restricted to the so-called 'great decade' of
1797–1807; Wordsworth wrote good poems, though less
frequently, till a very much later period, so the balance
has been kept as much as possible between earlier and later
work.

Most modern editors of selections have followed Arnold in
classifying the poems according to their form, narrative and
elegiac, lyrical, and so on. But Wordsworth's genius in every
form he handled is so peculiar and so closely related to his
sense of the living immediacy of his own experience

<blockquote>
the transitory being that beheld
This Vision,
</blockquote>

as he looks from the present moment back into the 'hiding
places' of his power, that only a chronological presentation is
really satisfactory. His own arrangement of the poems in 1815 in
terms of faculties of the mind, the Imagination, the Fancy, the
Affections, and so on, is rewarding when the poems are studied
in bulk but would prove tiresome in a short volume. His
classification has a serious weakness: it deviates into other
categories (Poems belonging to the Period of Old Age, Poems
of Childhood, etc.) so that, as someone remarked, it is reminiscent
of a butcher's shop in a university town which displayed the
sign 'University, Pork and Family Butcher'.

The critical reputation of Wordsworth has never stood higher;
yet the critics find it necessary to refer to an unproved and
probably ghostly neglect before saluting his genius. Certainly
prejudice or the fear of prejudice still lingers but it is apt to be
against the man rather than the poetry. The term Shakespearian
or Miltonist means a student of that particular poet; a Wordsworthian is a personal partisan. More than any other great
English poet except possibly Milton we are made aware as we
read him of the man behind the words. For many readers this

constitutes the principal difficulty in approaching his poetry. He possesses strength and integrity but not charm; not for instance the natural grace of Keats which reaches out into warm recognition of other human individualities. The oppressive shadow of a gigantic ego is thrust over us; the 'cold, hard, silent, practical man' obtrudes himself and his opinions, not indeed at the finest moments of his poetry but often in the poems where those finest moments occur.

The objection to Wordsworth's 'egotistical sublime' was first stated by Keats when he remarked: 'We hate poetry that has a palpable design upon us'. Even when stirred imaginatively by the poems so that our common experience is re-ordered we are uncomfortably conscious that they are not intended for our delight alone; as Mr. Norman Lacey says, 'Wordsworth provides the least purely poetic pleasure of any great English poet'; his song is tempered to philosophic and moral truth; he pipes a simple song for thinking hearts. This is not like Dante or Lucretius to let the song rise from a great structure of human thought so that the poetic architecture grows out of patterns of argument or schemes of cosmology, for this kind of philo-sophical poem can be accepted as a poem like any other, and our response to the final structure can be a purely literary one. But Wordsworth's 'thinking hearts' implies that he aims at setting us to think: like a sermon or a fable his songs, however simple, demand a degree of co-operation with the author's intention and personal beliefs not usually required from a poet's audience. Like their author the poems too are selfish, not trying to please, unwilling to concentrate on aesthetic delight, dwelling remorselessly and exhaustively within their own vision of the world.

The objection to Wordsworth's egoism can be met by a frank study of the poet's presentation of his experience. An egoist is not necessarily a bore; nor is Wordsworth a common-place egoist like Byron; his preoccupation with the moods of his own mind is soaring enough to make him feel that he has access to universal human experience: in reviewing

> The calm existence that is mine when I
> Am worthy of myself

he does not cease to tell us about ourselves. When the shock of recognition takes place his poetry has succeeded.

Our understanding of him must start out from a knowledge of his early life and development. This is not because our concern is with a romantic personality, or with the French Revolution, or with a philosophy of return to nature. It is because his poetry is chiefly about the mystery of being a person, of recollecting earlier phases of one's identity, of knowing other selves and the world in which one has being.

2. EARLY LIFE: THE GROWTH OF A POET

William Wordsworth was born at Cockermouth in Cumberland in 1770, the son of John Wordsworth, an attorney employed by Sir James Lowther, later Earl of Lonsdale. There were three other brothers and a sister, Dorothy. Wordsworth's favourite among his brothers was John who became a sailor in the merchant service. Between Wordsworth and his sister there was a close bond of affection from their earliest years. As a child he was moody and violent; he once struck his whip through a family portrait, and on another occasion in his grandfather's house he threatened to kill himself with one of the foils kept in the attic. His mother was anxious about him and declared that he alone of her children would be remarkable for good or evil. She was loving and sensible and allowed her children complete freedom to run wild on the banks of the Derwent which flowed below their home.

> Derwent, the fairest of all Rivers, loved
> To blend his murmurs with my Nurse's song,

> And from his alder shades and rocky falls,
> And from his fords and shallows, sent a voice
> That flow'd along my dreams.

His mother died in 1778 and William with his elder brother Richard was sent away to the grammar school at Hawkshead. Here again he enjoyed an extraordinary freedom to do what he liked outside the hours of work. Eighteenth-century schooling was very different from that of the next century, after the reform of the public school; boys were left much to their own devices; but Wordsworth's good fortune was exceptional. The boys were able in there free hours to wander over a wide expanse of the Lake country fishing, poaching, or riding. There was skating by starlight on their own lake of Esthwaite and midnight expeditions to Windermere. The foundation of all his later thinking about nature lies in these unconscious years. Their unheeding passion and joy could only be given a name by an adult looking back on them. The first two books of *The Prelude* bring his boyhood before us transfigured by the light of recollection. Wordsworth the child was not a queer little boy who pondered over the beauty of a tree or the exact nature of the thrill he was experiencing as he whirled round on his skates. It was the man who meditated and recollected. What the child did possess was an exceptionally strong animal sensibility and gifts of eye and ear which survived and developed. He describes how he would stand

> Beneath some rock, listening to sounds that are
> The ghostly language of the ancient earth,
> Or make their dim abode in distant winds.

The Prelude account goes on to analyse the training of the soul's faculties by these 'fleeting moods of shadowy exultation', but the original experience is simply one of strange and vivid excitement for which the terms 'fleeting', 'shadowy' and 'dim' are suitable epithets. Similarly he evokes another moment that

had remained imprinted on the memory: the dangerous thrill
of birds' nesting in the hills:

> Oh! when I have hung
> Above the raven's nest, by knots of grass
> And half-inch fissures in the slippery rock
> But ill-sustained and almost, as it seemed,
> Suspended by the blast which blew amain,
> Shouldering the naked crag,

before proceeding to examine the total harmony of the mind
which can blend together moments of terror and joy for its
own ends. The boy was innocent of the psychological refine-
ment of the young man; he possessed an infinite capacity for
feeling and enjoying, and his way of life bred a hardiness and
independence which never left him. Even as an old man he
remained the foremost skater on Rydal lake, and thought
nothing of walking fifteen miles to have tea with Southey and
back again; and he was capable of kicking over one of the
unmortared walls bounding land in the dales if it obstructed him
in the course of a ramble.

There was a darker side to Wordsworth's childhood of which
he says little in *The Prelude*. John Wordsworth died in the
winter of 1783, leaving his children to the guardianship of his
brother Richard and their mother's uncle, Christopher Crackan-
thorpe Cookson. The Earl of Lonsdale, an almost maniacal
tyrant, had withheld money due to his agent and left loans
from him unrepaid. He owed the Wordsworth estate about
£4,700, and by retaining all the best counsel consistently balked
the efforts of the family to recover their patrimony through the
courts. It was not until 1802 that the debt was repaid with interest
by his successor and William and Dorothy came into their
own. The young Wordsworths lived for most of the time with
their grandparents, the Cooksons, in their draper's shop in
Penrith. Until the debt was paid their prospects were meagre
and there were members of the household who were not averse

to reminding them of this. The self-willed William seems to have got on particularly badly with his grandfather. He was separated from Dorothy who went to live with a cousin at Halifax. Apart from a reference to 'early miseries, regrets, vexations' nothing is said of this change of circumstances in *The Prelude*, but it must have exerted a profound effect on the boy's sensitive temperament. The contact with upper class oppression prepared him for the acceptance of revolutionary sentiments later:

> I nothing found
> Then, or had ever, even in crudest youth,
> That dazzled me; but rather what my soul
> Mourned for, or loathed, beholding that the best
> Rul'd not, and feeling that they ought to rule.

His upbringing had been among the scattered farmers of the Westmorland dales, who were almost all independent small-holders; the people among whom he moved did not look up to a squire or down upon the village poor; in that 'almost visionary republic of the mountains' he saw no one who was vested with respect through claims of wealth or blood. His schoolfellows were farmers' sons talking in the broad speech of Westmorland, like the boy who asked him: 'How is it, Bill, thee doest write such good verses? Doest thee invoke Muses?'. Wordsworth retained a strong northern accent all his life. But although his environment gave him a healthy distrust of pride and privilege, he was not able to enter into the everyday concerns of the people of the Lakes as Burns could do with his fellow Lowland Scots. He could admire the fine integrity of the shepherds striding through the mist 'in shape like Greenland bears'; he could not talk with them about the small joys and sorrows of life. He had his good friends like John Fleming of Rayrigg with whom he used to walk round the lake of Esthwaite before breakfast, but there was something austere and unsocial about his temperament.

In October 1787 he was sent by his guardians to St. John's College, Cambridge, with which the family had a connection. Clearly four years at the university were going to make severe inroads on the already hard-pressed estate; the attitude of the Cooksons towards William was, as we learn from Dorothy's letters, far from kindly, and they must have expected from Cambridge the acquirement of a profession which would settle a youth who was becoming more and more difficult. But in the next few years Wordsworth consistently opposed all attempts to make him decide upon a career. He first aimed at the law but soon gave it up. Then it was hoped that he would go into the church or become a private tutor. He kept his guardians guessing by a policy of deliberate stalling. He read what he liked, and what he liked was the English poets, and some Italian, Spanish and French; he found mathematics too dry and neglected many parts of the subject. The consequence was that in 1790 he had given up all thoughts of obtaining a fellowship. Another avenue was closed to him.

If Wordsworth wasted his time at Cambridge it was with good precedent, exploring the surfaces of artificial life, 'reading lazily in lazy books', and altogether giving himself up to 'strenuous idleness'. He felt unhappy about this period afterwards because he felt he did not really belong to the place or the time. What he says in a letter about his stay in London later could be applied to the whole undergraduate period: he had the sensation of being thrown by an eddy into a corner of the stream where he lay in almost motionless indolence. He experienced no ordinary remorse on account of his idleness (indeed the letters of his youth breathe a rather frighteningly cold and arrogant self-assurance) but only

> A feeling that I was not for that hour,
> Nor for that place.

It was however in this period that he first began seriously to write poetry. Before he went to the university he had already composed a rambling poem in octosyllabic couplets about the surrounding countryside (*The Vale of Esthwaite*), a strange mixture of conventional eighteenth-century landscape verse and ghost story in the Gothic manner. Now in his vacations from Cambridge he began to use this material for a more orderly landscape poem in heroic couplets (*An Evening Walk*). The shock of his first separation from the known and the familiar stirred him into being a poet. He wrote of what was absent because, in a whirl of novelties, it was a way of assuring himself that he was still the same person; the reality of the loved absent sights of Esthwaite and Grasmere was now something he carried about in his mind; it increased his own sense of personal integration and helped to banish the uneasy mood

> when foresight sleeps,
> And wisdom, and the pledges interchanged
> With our own inner being are forgot.

All his major poetry was to be written in these circumstances: either in separation from the place or the person he was writing about, or on a return to the original scene after a period of separation. Thus *The Prelude*, the story of his early life, was begun in Germany at a time when he and his sister were enduring the pains of homesickness; the first part of *The Recluse* was written after returning to live in the vale of Grasmere after nine years away from the Lakes; in *Tintern Abbey* Wordsworth recalls an earlier visit to the same spot and by describing how much his thoughts and emotions have changed contrives to suggest the essential unity of the developing soul and the sympathy connecting it with the universal scheme of things; and the Scottish and continental tours of his later days would often hurry him into his singing robes *after* he had returned home, when the object was already visible suitably distanced and shaped in the frame of recollection.

In the long vacation of 1790, instead of reading for his

forthcoming degree, he went on a three months' walking tour through France, Italy and Switzerland with a friend, Robert Jones. It was hard going: with bundles on their backs they averaged about twenty miles a day. They crossed the Alps by the Simplon Pass and only learnt that they had done so when, after wandering off the track, they asked a peasant the way. It was one of the moments the poet was to return to as a type of the human imagination confronted by the mystery of the universe:

> Effort, and expectation, and desire,
> And something evermore about to be.

In France they had seen the Revolution in full spate. They had arrived on the anniversary of the fall of the Bastille and joined in celebrations and dances of liberty:

> France standing on the top of golden hours,
> And human nature seeming born again.

But Wordsworth was not yet intimately touched by the Revolution; he took the joy for granted as another aspect of the joy he felt among the mountains.

He took his degree in January 1791. For four more years he wavered and put off the choice of a profession until a piece of good luck gave him a modest independence and made the choice unnecessary. Meanwhile he was writing poetry but he had not found himself as a poet.

Descriptive Sketches, a desultory poem on Alpine life and scenery, was published with *An Evening Walk* in 1793. In both poems he employs the established diction of eighteenth-century descriptive verse which aimed at a pictorial effect: the scene was enclosed in a frame with appropriate background and middle distance; Wordsworth was trying to communicate through a basically objective and therefore unresponsive medium a vision of natural objects which was becoming increasingly subjective.

One purpose that he kept steadily in mind was an ultimate reunion with Dorothy. They had met only for brief intervals since the family had broken up. It was necessary for him to make some show of compliance with the wishes of his guardians while gaining time. Probably for this reason he went to France again in the winter of 1791, ostensibly to learn the language more perfectly so as to fit himself as a private tutor to a rich man's son. He stayed at Orleans and moved in the spring to Blois. There he became involved in a double love affair, with a girl, and with the republican cause; with both there were no reservations. The girl Annette Vallon was the daughter of a surgeon at Blois; the family were of royalist sympathies. In December 1792 she bore him a daughter, Caroline. The outbreak of war with France separated the lovers and gradually destroyed their hopes of marriage; he made payments to Annette for the education of their daughter until her marriage. His family and intimate friends knew about the relationship. The suppression of the facts in his lifetime and their omission from his auto-biography were probably in deference to Annette and her family, not to puritan censorship. The young Wordsworth was an eighteenth-century man and a man of strong passions. The fuss made about Annette by modern biographers is based on a fundamental misconception; it would be more to the point to ask the question why he did not have more illegitimate daughters. This was clearly no casual entanglement; lines in the uneven *Vaudracour and Julia* which refers obliquely to his love for Annette are a touchstone of intense romantic passion

> Earth lived in one great presence of the spring . . .
>   all paradise
> Could by the simple opening of a door
> Let itself in upon him.

It is wrong to minimize the importance of Annette Vallon in

Wordsworth's development. The love affair aroused in him a human tenderness in which he had been signally lacking; the poems of the next ten years are full of distressed and abandoned creatures with only their humanity to preserve them, predominant among them the figure of the abandoned mother with her child; as the bond with Annette weakened, her poetic influence became more fertile, and she became a window on to a world of devoted outcasts like Margaret waiting with hopeless patience at the door of the ruined cottage for the husband who never comes. It is also wrong to exaggerate the problematic psychological disturbance caused to Wordsworth; his imagination cannot have been blighted by remorse since he managed to write his greatest, and some of his most radiantly optimistic poetry, after his stay in France.

Romantic passion was mingled with political enthusiasm and each took fresh fire from the other. Again communion was achieved through a person, Michel Beaupuy, an officer of the garrison at Blois, and a republican in a largely royalist mess. The natural democracy of the mountains was now reinforced by the theory of the rights of man. Wordsworth seems to have given his active support to the party of the Gironde or moderates, and if he had not returned to England at the end of 1792, 'compelled by want of funds', he might have run into danger in the forthcoming Terror.

In February 1793 Pitt's government declared war against France. It was a devastating blow to Wordsworth. Not only was he separated from Annette but he found himself, since his loyalty to the Revolution was undiminished, a potential traitor in his own country. In spite of his arrogance he was always a man to whom the sense of having his roots in a community was more comforting than it is to most people; now he was uprooted. Other young radical intellectuals of the day suffered the same shock but few were plunged into the agony of self-conflict endured by Wordsworth:

> Not in my single self alone I found,
> But in the minds of all ingenuous Youth,
> Change and subversion from this hour.

His distress was increased by the imperialist policy of the French republic. After 1939 some left-wing intellectuals disillusioned by the policy of Stalinism sought relief in the doctrine of Trotsky or in anarchism: the revolution had not failed, it was simply postponed. Wordsworth similarly turned for a time to the ideas of the philosopher William Godwin (*Political Justice*, 1793): man was infinitely perfectible if he brought a dispassionate reason to bear on the traditions and institutions which shackled him; the self-cultivation of the individual would bring in the millenium. Such intellectualism was against the grain of his temperament and upbringing. In his only drama, *The Borderers*, a not unimpressive closet play derivative from Shakespearian tragedy, he explores the moral horrors that lie in wait for Godwinian man trying to dispense with any sense of sin or universal justice.

Though theoretical Godwinianism was an unfortunate deviation from the true line of his development which he later rejected, Wordsworth formed another allegiance in this obscure phase of moral crisis which was to remain a permanent source of strength. He turned to the common people for instances of the universal human integrity underlying the sophistications of class and education; he was especially interested in those outside the pale of civil society, beggars, people driven to crime by want, the very old, and those crazed by suffering. It seems probable that a large part of the mature Wordsworth's attitude to the healing power of nature and to the elemental virtue of the poor countryman was coming to the surface in this period of which so little is known and should not be attributed so exclusively to the later influence of Coleridge and Dorothy. For it was not all gloom and moral crisis in these years. The great dithyramb of joy which begins *The Prelude* was probably composed in 1795.

3. THE CREATIVE YEARS

In January 1795 a single stroke of fortune brought a pause in the years of anxious, restless wandering and enabled Wordsworth to realize his cherished ambition to set up house with Dorothy. Raisley Calvert, a friend who had died of consumption, and whom he had nursed during his last illness, left him a legacy of £900. He and his sister were able to live frugally on an annuity bought with the money until the Lonsdale heir paid his debts in 1802. After a last spell of indecision in London, where he toyed with the idea of starting a radical newspaper, Wordsworth accepted the offer of a rent-free house at Racedown in Dorset. He and Dorothy lived there from September 1795 till July 1797. Before settling at Racedown he met Coleridge at a political meeting in Bristol, and the two quickly became close friends. Eventually the Wordsworths moved to Alfoxden, a large house in the wooded coombes of the Quantocks overlooking the Bristol Channel, in order to be near Coleridge and his wife who were living three miles away in a cottage in the village of Nether Stowey. There for a year the three friends (for Mrs. Coleridge could never enter the charmed circle—she was not a feeder on honeydew) enjoyed an almost daily communion of walks and talks and exchange of poetry and ideas. It was a collaboration so intense and extraordinary as not to permit any precise disentanglement of who owed what and to whom. Most important of all for Wordsworth was the simple fact of the recognition of his genius by another poet at a crucial stage of his creative life; Coleridge's generous, unselfish discipleship was his chief gift; if his metaphysical enthusiasm encouraged Wordsworth to organize his insights more systematically or to contemplate a great philosophical poem, it was a less valuable contribution on his part. Dorothy brought to the partnership a sensitiveness to every aspect of nature: her superbly direct and unromanticized perception of the natural cycle is recorded in her *Alfoxden Journal;* it found its way, in odd phrases and observations, into many poems by both Wordsworth and Coleridge. Really it is as if the movement of the year from winter to summer in 1798 at Alfoxden was itself an element in the collaboration. The late spring, the withered leaves dancing on the trees, a dog baying, the crescent moon settling behind cloud, are carried over from their mere reporting in the *Journal* into the imaginative life of the ballad poems the two poets wrote.

The poems begun at Racedown, *Salisbury Plain* and *The Ruined Cottage* (later called *The Pedlar* and finally incorporated in the first book of *The Excursion*) demonstrate for the first time the characteristic Wordsworthian manner: an austerity of style which is not afraid of the prosaic since the poet sees in verbal commonplace a reflection of the human emotions which survive and have moral value. The earlier poems had preserved the rather theatrical declamatory manner of eighteenth-century landscape verse; the new, flat tone, since it does not draw attention to an egoistic poet making poetry out of pathetic incidents, allows a much greater degree of identification with the suffering individual; the figure of the bereaved Margaret is convincing through this inwardness with the character and through the deployment of significant detail. When Coleridge heard the poems read by Wordsworth in June 1797, he detected this new quality and wrote later of 'the union of deep feeling with profound thought; the fine balance of truth in observing with the imaginative faculty in modifying the objects observed; and above all the original gift of spreading the tone, the *atmosphere*, and with it the depth and height of the ideal world around forms, incidents and situations, of which, for the common view, custom had bedimmed all the lustre, had dried up the sparkle and the dew drops'.

From admiration the two poets turned to collaboration. In November 1797, on a long walking tour to Lynton in

Somerset, they planned to write a poem for *The New Monthly Magazine* which would defray their expenses. The poem was *The Ancient Mariner*. After contributing the idea of the mariner's persecution by the tutelary spirits of the South Seas, and a few phrases, Wordsworth soon realized that he had no aptitude for the imaginative treatment of the supernatural. The project changed to one for a joint volume in which, while Coleridge devoted himself to endowing supernatural subjects with human interest, Wordsworth in the poems which fell to his share was to 'give the charm of novelty to things of every day, and to excite a feeling analogous to the supernatural, by awakening the mind's attention from the lethargy of custom'. About the same time Wordsworth composed in *Peter Bell* his own version of *The Ancient Mariner*; like the latter poem it is the story of an alienated and guilty soul purged and restored to unity with his fellow men by the shock of extraordinary occurrences, but with an almost teasing care every melodramatic incident is traced to a natural cause. What the poem (together with many of Wordsworth's other contributions to *Lyrical Ballads*) has in common with *The Ancient Mariner* is a concern with the feelings of the simple or primitive mind as an assurance of the primacy of an eternal standard of right and wrong, of the holiness of the heart's affections, and not some mere principle of utility brought into being by man's passive adaptation to his environment. It was this impulse which led both Wordsworth and Coleridge to devour avidly books of travels and the descriptions of savage peoples. One of Wordsworth's stark little ballads shows us Harry Gill as the victim of a curse on account of his guilty conscience: he has wronged the old woman who then professes to put a spell upon him, and then the witchcraft actually becomes effective and he cannot feel warm again. Wordsworth is not at all interested in making his reputed witch an awe-inspiring figure; she is a poor homely body, because, unlike Coleridge, he has a hard-headed eighteenth-century attitude to that sort of thing; his interest is purely psychological. The mind is master of the body and can accomplish strange things; there is a poetic justice in the treatment of Peter Bell and Harry Gill: conversion and moral reproof are brought about by natural processes.

As spring came to the countryside around Alfoxden Wordsworth observed it lovingly, reverting to the simple joyousness of his boyhood. A new strain of optimism appears in the lyrics of 1798:

> Love, now an universal birth,
> From heart to heart is stealing,
> From earth to man, from man to earth:
> —It is the hour of feeling.
>
> One moment now may give us more
> Than years of toiling reason:
> Our minds shall drink at every pore
> The spirit of the season.

His interest in the outcasts of society, the solitary and suffering, continued and developed; but he now begins to suggest that the natural world to which their plight has brought them so close may provide for them a special kind of comfort. The Old Cumberland Beggar is reduced like this; he is more a part of the landscape than a member of the human family:

> he is so still
> In look and motion, that the cottage curs,
> Ere he has passed the door, will turn away,
> Weary of barking at him.
>
> deem him not
> A burthen of the earth! 'Tis nature's law
> That none, the meanest of created things,
> Of forms created the most vile and brute,
> The dullest or most noxious, should exist
> Divorced from good—a spirit and pulse of good,
> A life and soul, to every mode of being
> Inseparably linked.

Two other classes of people allied to the solitaries are cele-brated in the *Lyrical Ballads*. They are children and those de-ranged in mind (his interest in the latter provided a sitting target for the hard-boiled wits of the reviews). Both groups were for different reasons unenslaved by the 'meddling intellect'. The little girl who says 'We are seven' understands the nature of family love more deeply than the quibbling adult who points out that if a brother and sister are sleeping in the churchyard then there must be only five. And the distracted woman in *The Thorn* is both a solitary and a person enfeebled in mind by her sufferings. Wordsworth shows a keen psychological interest in the workings of insanity and in the child mind. At Alfoxden he and Dorothy were bringing up in a progressive fashion the son of a friend, Basil Montagu, and interest in an education which should be enlightened but not cranky was reinforced by practical experience. But the most important result of this interest in education was that it took him back for comparison to his own early life; in seeking how an individual might grow to his full mental and emotional stature in a balanced, natural environment, and without the artificial stimulus of text-book education, Wordsworth was led to ponder the good fortune of his own upbringing and to contemplate a poem on his own development in which the philosophic and autobio-graphical would be combined. He was already planning, at the encouragement of Coleridge, a long philosophical poem to be called *The Recluse: or, Views of Man, Nature and Society*. Before he could settle down to it he found he had to examine afresh the growth of his poetic personality; the result of this was *The Prelude, or the Growth of a Poet's Mind*, which he designed as an introduction to the larger work. The latter was never com-pleted: as has been said, all that was written was a *Prelude* to the main theme and an *Excursion* from it (*The Excursion*, forming the second part of the whole work, was published in 1814; *The Prelude* remained in manuscript until his death).

A vivid account of Wordsworth's appearance at this time is given by Hazlitt who as an impressionable young man, full of poetry and libertarian politics and theology, visited the Alfoxden household to pay homage to Coleridge. 'There was something of a roll, a lounge in his gait . . . a severe, worn pressure of thought about his temples, a fire in his eye (as if he saw something in objects more than the outward appearance), an intense, high, narrow forehead, a Roman nose, cheeks furrowed by strong purpose and feeling, and a convulsive inclination to laughter about the mouth, a good deal at variance with the solemn, stately expression of the rest of his face. . . .'

The *annus mirabilis* came to an end in July because the trustee of Alfoxden, Mrs. St. Aubyn, was not willing to renew the lease. She may have listened to the local gossip which made out that Coleridge and the Wordsworths were Jacobin agents. There were even stories of their discussing a fellow agent, a certain 'Spy Nosey' (Spinoza), which brought a security man down from London. The friends had to endure the same petty persecution which fell to D. H. Lawrence and his wife Frieda in the 1914–18 war, but they were too robust and too full of their own concerns to care about it as Lawrence did. The Wordsworths went to Bristol to see *Lyrical Ballads* through the press; during their stay they made a tour on foot and by boat up the Wye valley to Tintern. At Tintern Abbey Wordsworth recalled his visit there five years before in the tumultuous period of his revolutionary enthusiasm when war with France had lately broken out; he meditated on the new quality he had found in nature since that time, and as was usual with him, meditation led to improvisation. Verses were forming in his head as he walked and sailed back to their lodgings near Bristol. The poem was written down, probably at Cottle the publisher's, and added to the volume already set up in type. *Tintern Abbey* with its personal framework and elevated style is very different from the lyrical ballads proper: it looks forward to the impassioned but conscientiously introspective poetry of *The Prelude* and is an admirable introduction to that work.

In September, on the eve of the publication of the volume, Wordsworth left for Germany with Dorothy and Coleridge. The thrill of the new German romantic poetry and the transcendental philosophy was just beginning to be felt; like all geniuses Wordsworth and Coleridge were anticipating the fashion of a generation or more later when Heidelberg and Göttingen should become the intellectual lodestars of Europe. The German tour was the final phase of the rootless, restless wandering in which Wordsworth had indulged on and off since 1790. He and his sister had now no home or family ties; Coleridge had left behind him a wife who was going to have a baby. After arriving in Hamburg and visiting the old German poet Klopstock, who shocked them by preferring the blank verse of the eighteenth-century poetaster Glover to that of Milton, they separated. Coleridge went on to Ratzeburg and then to Göttingen where he feasted on metaphysics and acquired a good working knowledge of the German language. Wordsworth and Dorothy proceeded to Goslar, a humdrum little town on the north German plain, where they endured the coldest winter for a century in an almost total absence of society. Neither had the ready charm of manner which procured for Coleridge friends and listeners wherever he went. They were driven in on themselves and on common memories of their old home and the Lakes which became increasingly nostalgic:

> I travelled among unknown men,
> In lands beyond the sea;
> Nor, England! did I know till then
> What love I bore to thee.

Turning back to his boyhood Wordsworth now saw his early moments of awe and excitement in the face of nature suffused by a luminous glory; to the exile of thirty who had travelled so far they were signposts and tokens of his identity; since he could respond to them now in recollection with something like the same love and excitement they were proof of the dignity of the human spirit and that his life was a unified pattern, not a succession of meaningless moments of experience. In a mood of fruitful nostalgia he wrote some of his best work. Much of the first two books of *The Prelude* was composed, including the description of skating and that of the stolen boat on Ullswater. Many shorter poems were also written which were published in the second edition of *Lyrical Ballads* in 1800, among them the Lucy series. It is idle to speculate about the identity of Lucy[1], since this is not autobiographical love poetry but an idealized portrait of the child of nature:

> She dwelt among the untrodden ways
> Beside the springs of Dove,
> A Maid whom there were none to praise
> And very few to love.

The tone is strangely sexless. Wordsworth often in his poems transferred incidents and combined characters. Some of his feeling for his sister undoubtedly went into the poems; he may also have been remembering the early death of Margaret (Peggy) Hutchinson, the sister of the girl he was to marry. But the elusive mystery of Lucy, which is after all one main quality of the poems, is not solved when these suggestions have been noted. The mystery is clothed in a verbal statement most daring in its sheer simplicity; it is quite different from the rustic, repetitive simplicity of many of the ballads which was intended to convey the outlook of an uneducated narrator.

The late summer was spent with their friends the Hutchinsons at their farm at Sockburn on the Tees. Mary Hutchinson had been a childhood friend. Wordsworth now began to fall in love with her. Separation had killed his affection for Annette,

[1] Ingenious attempts to identify her have lately been made by Mr. F. W. Bateson in *Wordsworth: a Re-Interpretation* (2nd. ed. 1956) and H. M. Margoliouth in *Wordsworth and Coleridge, 1795–1834* (1951).

but not his loyalty to her: when he married Mary two years later he not only settled an allowance on his former lover but went to see her before the wedding, making a journey to Calais for the purpose in the brief interval afforded by the Peace of Amiens.

The years of wandering were nearly over. In coming north again Wordsworth had drawn near to his origins and he could not resist the impulse to return to the source; on a tour from Sockburn into the Lake district with Coleridge and his sailor brother John he rediscovered the secluded and beautiful vale of Grasmere which he had known as a schoolboy, exploring over the hills from Hawkshead:

> As beautiful to thought, as it had been
> When present to the bodily sense.

He found a cottage there and took Dorothy to it at the end of December 1799 across the snow-clad Pennines:

> the naked trees
> The icy brooks, as on we passed, appeared
> To question us, 'Whence come ye? to what end?'

He was ready to settle down at a younger age than most poets are. In him the capacity for passionate feeling was matched by a need for stability and the background of a quiet common life; and he had almost finished taking in new experience: the intense emotional life of his early years was succeeded by a great calm.

The cottage he had taken at Town-end had once been an inn called the Dove and Olive Branch and it came to be called Dove Cottage. The years 1800–2 were busy and productive if without the miraculous quality of those that had just passed. Coleridge followed 'his god Wordsworth' to the north; he was also drawn by love for Sara Hutchinson, Mary's sister; he was unhappy with his wife and his frustrated passion for Sara Hutchinson was to make him miserable for years. He and his wife came to live at Greta Hall, Keswick, in July 1800. Wordsworth wrote a defence and explanation of his experiments in simple diction in *Lyrical Ballads* and this famous Preface was published in the second edition of 1800. In 1802 it was considerably revised. Once more he was able to talk over his ideas almost daily with Coleridge, so that afterwards the latter could say 'The Preface is half a child of my own brain'. Wordsworth's rather vague account of his purpose as an attempt to describe common incidents 'in a selection of language really used by men', and his theory that there was no essential difference between the language of prose and that of poetry, led him into a number of difficulties. But his main point, that poetry must bear some relation to common speech, and must in its aims not be merely light entertainment (a literary taste being, as he says, viewed only like a taste for sherry) but must speak of the deepest human concerns, is the foundation of all our later thinking about poetry: in Wordsworth's fine phrase the poet is 'a man speaking to men'. The poet can extend humanity's knowledge of its own nature, marching step by step with the scientist who pushes back the frontiers of physical knowledge: poetry is 'the impassioned expression which is in the countenance of all Science . . . the Poet binds together by passion and knowledge the vast empire of human society'. Illuminating too in its application to his own practice is the famous statement that 'Poetry takes its origin from emotion recollected in tranquillity'.

At Grasmere more books were available and Wordsworth read more. He read the older English poets, Chaucer and Milton and the Elizabethans, and his work began to show a greater metrical variety and to lose the unliterary starkness and deliberate bathos of his earlier phase. These poems, collected in the *Poems in Two Volumes* of 1807, show that Wordsworth had come home not only to Grasmere but to the main tradition of English poetry. But he still liked to compose extempore, pacing the walk near his house. Some of these fine poems, *Michael*,

Resolution and Independence, The Brothers, still celebrate the virtues of simple endurance and isolation, but the solitaries have now achieved some sort of happy compromise with society; indeed to some extent their heroism and wisdom is made possible by the permanent habits of a rural community. In *Michael* Wordsworth is celebrating the Lakeland republic of upright, God-fearing shepherds as well as the heroic individual.

4. MIDDLE AND LATER YEARS

In the ensuing years Wordsworth bound himself more firmly by the normal bonds of marriage and children to the English society he had grown to accept. After travelling with Dorothy to meet Annette at Calais, he was married to Mary Hutchinson in October 1802. The only cloud over these years was provided by the illness and personal troubles of Coleridge. If all was outwardly calm, however, Wordsworth had reached a crisis in his poetic life, a crisis marked by the *Ode* (later called *Ode on the Intimations of Immortality from Recollections of Early Childhood*) which he had begun to compose in the early summer of 1802. The *Ode* marks a definite recognition that the period of careless joy in nature was drawing to a close; his years of taking in were over and he looked forward with melancholy insight to the decline of his creative powers:

Whither is fled the visionary gleam?

The moments of visionary awareness (such as he describes in *Tintern Abbey* and the last of the Lucy poems) in which he seemed to lose himself completely, were becoming less frequent. Soon he would only have the rich store of his memories to rely on:

O joy! that in our embers
Is something that doth live,
That nature yet remembers
What was so fugitive!

xxxiii

A price had to be paid, too, for his acceptance of the world of daily life with all its responsibilities; the wild child of nature who fled from obligations had become the married man with a small stake in the country; the Jacobin had turned into the conservative patriot who wrote in this summer sonnets of splendid severity against the corruptions of his countrymen and the threat from infidel France. Too often critics of Wordsworth have seen this change in his attitude as simple betrayal or decay. It would be truer to say that he was facing that crisis of mature life which comes to most men; he was living through it more honestly than most, and in poems like the *Ode* rendering the crisis in literary terms, a very rare achievement indeed. Those are fortunate who have visions and beliefs to become blurred, and Wordsworth felt the agony of their becoming blurred more keenly than the majority; above all he never ceased trying to keep a sense of continuity with the child and the young visionary who seemed increasingly far away. His inclination towards tradition and family piety (Anglicanism came in later as a prop for an almost Virgilian *pietas*) sprang from the desire to keep hold of his personal past and ground it in something strong and permanent:

> I could wish that all our days should be
> Bound each to each by natural piety.

His re-encounter with Annette on the sea-shore at Calais, with Dorothy, and with the 'dear child' who was the daughter he had never seen before, may be one of the more curious meetings of literary history; but it is an episode not without human dignity.

In the autumn of 1803, a few months after the birth of the first child of his marriage, he went on a walking tour in Scotland with Dorothy, visiting the Highlands and meeting Sir Walter Scott who remained a life-long friend. Coleridge accompanied them only on the early stages of the tour. *The Solitary Reaper*,

To a Highland Girl, Stepping Westward and other poems were the fruit of this journey; it was the last occasion on which Wordsworth was to gain a store of vital fresh impressions; many of the verses he brought back from his later continental tours are little more than dutiful comments in the margin of a guide book.

Work on his *magnum opus*, *The Recluse*, was held up in these years, partly because of the absence in Malta of Coleridge on whom Wordsworth depended for help with the philosophical portions. But a more important reason why he only left fragments of his 'views on man, nature, and society' was that all the life-blood of the work flowed into *The Prelude*; in spite of his great will he lacked the concentration to achieve a long work of a more objective nature; his energetic sensibility dissipated itself in a multitude of impressions treated in an equal number of shorter poems. They were to be the little shrines and chapels round the huge Gothic nave of the long poem. However, only a few pillars of the nave were raised. Wordsworth was a profound psychologist but he could not reason in verse except about the phenomena of his own mind. The section which was completed and published in 1814, *The Excursion*, is an attempt to project the conflict between the different phases of his personality into a group of characters, the Solitary (the disillusioned revolutionary who has desperately experimented with human nature), the Wanderer (the idealized countryman taking strength from the mountains), and the Pastor (his newly found Christian faith). *The Prelude* was finished in its original version in 1805–6 and read to Coleridge in January 1807. Though it was not published in his lifetime Wordsworth continuously revised the poem; even when he brought in approving references to Burke and to college chapel, opinions which were certainly not his in his undergraduate days, it was a form of honesty; the work had to be made to conform to the full range of his personal interests at the moment: the child was father of the man. The later version also has some fine additional lines and shows a general improvement in elegance and continuity. But the roughness of style in the early text is often a merit; the task the poet had undertaken required that, in Pound's phrase, he should 'stammer with simple speech': if he uses what seem to the purist to be too many double negatives it is because it is so hard to be sure what an important incident in one's mental progress was *really* like and yet the effort must be made. As for faithfulness to the facts of his early development, there is no question that the 1805 text (as it is usually called) is the better of the two.

Various events combined to darken with grief and anxiety the middle years of Wordsworth's life. His favourite brother, John, was drowned at sea in 1805. Both Wordsworth and Dorothy were for a time overwhelmed by the blow; 'I can never again have a *perfect*—that is an unchastized—joy in this world' wrote the latter. Like Tennyson later in *In Memoriam*, a personal loss drove Wordsworth to think deeply about survival beyond the grave; for the first time he began to direct his rather vague spirituality towards an orthodox Christian hope; his submission to dogma is a practical step designed to gain for himself peace of mind:

> Me this unchartered freedom tires;
> I feel the weight of chance-desires:
> My hopes no more must change their name,
> I long for a repose that ever is the same.

A certain hard stoic nobility emerges in his attitude to duty and suffering in the poems written about this time (*Ode to Duty*, *Elegiac Stanzas*) and in the passive resignation of the heroine of *The White Doe of Rylstone* (written in 1807) when her whole family is destroyed for a cause in which she does not believe. Getting the better of circumstances and of his natural vein of melancholy Wordsworth weathered the storm of these years; he developed a protective armour of conventional behaviour, country gentleman's Toryism. His Anglicanism was more than a mere crust: there are deeply felt poems in the *Ecclesiastical Sketches* (1822).

The story of the last forty years can be briefly told. Apart from occasional triumphant visits to London for talk with Lamb and other friends, Wordsworth lived increasingly within his family circle, fostered and protected by a number of able women who copied out his poems and respectfully criticized them; his wife, Sara Hutchinson, and Dorothy were the chief of these, and later his favourite daughter Dora. The legend of the barrenness of Wordsworth's later years dies hard. *The Excursion* (1814) and the still more neglected *The White Doe of Rylstone* (1815) are both major achievements; the discontent with the later Wordsworth of Keats, Shelley and their generation was due to what they believed was his surrender to political reaction and his dogmatic hardness in pressing his opinions; Keats greatly admired *The Excursion* and did not consider that it revealed a poetic decline. Into old age the poet remained shrewd and sensible in defending his views on political and social matters, and often astonishingly far-seeing, as for instance in his judgments on the advance of democracy or on scientific progress. He often found himself on the side of the Tories because he came to see that the alliance of Reform and the new manufacturing interests would destroy and not assist his dream of the organic community. Even the years after 1820 still saw some magnificent poetry. His tardy, somewhat grudging acceptance of the Christian consolation as if it were but the religion of the country which must be taken on with the other civic responsibilities of middle life now deepened into a full enjoyment of the sacramental view of nature; this gave a new dimension to his earlier creed. There is a bolder use of symbolism: the scenes the eye beholds are not described for their immediate beauty but as types of eternity. This is after all a logical development of the earlier view; Wordsworth in his great phase never regards the stupendous shock of natural beauty as a source of mere aesthetic enjoyment; it is an imperfect means of access to the mystery of things. As early as the lines on the Simplon Pass (1799; p. 12) he speaks of the awesome impressions of Alpine scenery as

> blossoms upon one tree,
> Characters of the great Apocalypse,
> The types and symbols of Eternity,
> Of first and last, and midst, and without end.

The River Duddon sonnets and the *Ecclesiastical Sketches* contain magnificent work in this vein. I have chosen one sonnet from each series, and another poem *Processions* to represent this phase of Wordsworth's art.

Wordsworth preserved his faculties to the end of his long life. Younger friends and children predeceased him; the *Extempore Effusion* of 1835 is a poignant, clear-eyed lament over those who had left him, Coleridge among them, 'the rapt one of the god-like forehead'. He accepted the Laureateship, after a first refusal, in 1843, succeeding his friend Southey. When he died at the age of eighty in 1850 fame had caught up with him and even his long life had become a part of literature.

5. WORDSWORTH THE POET

Wordsworth is not an easy poet to represent adequately in selections. An editor has a huge body of poems to select from, which are apparently uneven in quality and yet ultimately homogeneous. Critics from Matthew Arnold to Mr. F. W. Bateson have tried to distinguish the 'Two Voices' of his poetry, the sublime trumpet note and the bleat 'as of an old, half-witted sheep' (J. K. Stephen). If the banal Wordsworth was simply bleating, it would be easy, but the daring simplicity is often successful and makes impossible a neat classification on these lines. The chaff can easily be separated from the wheat in other voluminous poets, Tennyson or Browning for instance, and little of value be lost. But when Wordsworth fails to communicate he is using the same method with language that he employs in his universally accepted masterpieces; we can never be sure that it is not we who have failed, as readers, to detect an important purpose, and to conform to that ideal audience, free from stock responses about conventionally pleasing diction, for which he was always hoping.

All his poems can be regarded as offshoots of *The Prelude*. They represent a single attempt to explore in its freshness the world in which man finds himself and to understand the energies which move it; he strives to preserve the innocent eye of childhood and then to communicate the mature experience of the man, still keeping faith with his past, without sophistication or abstraction. More than most great poets he had a contempt for literature, if by literature is meant the verbal decoration of a theme and the creation of an aesthetic object for its own sake. He always has his eye on the object. It may be a piece of concrete observation, and for this his senses were as finely developed as those of any more sensuous, less reflective, poet. He gives us the sound of skating:

> All shod with steel,
> We hissed along the polished ice. . . .
> The leafless trees, and every icy crag
> Tinkled like iron.

or a detail of visual observation:

> The Hare is running races in her mirth;
> And with her feet she from the plashy earth
> Raises a mist.

> Clothed in the sunshine of the withering fern.

Or it may be a description where the different senses are subtly fused:

> A soft eye-music of slow-waving boughs.

> The immeasurable height
> Of woods decaying, never to be decayed,
> The stationary blasts of waterfalls. . . .

Unlike the general run of descriptive poets who are satisfied if they achieve a static, pictorial effect (we think of Keats) Wordsworth can direct his gifts of eye and ear and touch to conveying a sense of the energy and movement behind the workings of the natural world; 'goings on' was a favourite word of his applied to nature; he looks beyond the landscape to the solid, geological masses of the mountains, and beyond them to the stars moving in their courses:

> Rolled round in earth's diurnal course
> With rocks, and stones, and trees.

What other poet would imagine the dead Lucy drawn into the planetary motion of the universe? He can make poetry out of astronomy and fulfil his own programme for the poet of marching step by step with the man of science.

But he is not interested in mere nature writing. To describe the object without giving his own thoughts about it would be just as much an act of abstraction as to record his own feelings without any reference to the objects which stimulated and called them forth. His eye is on the original experience in which the object seen, the mountain towering above the frightened little boy in the boat, is inseparable from his feelings about it. Still he tries, with this more complex thing to say, to be honest and objective, even if a visionary excitement is to be communicated. If he is not quite sure what it all meant he says so:

> Oh! at that time,
> While on the perilous ridge I hung alone
> With what strange utterance did the loud dry wind
> Blow through my ears! the sky seemed not a sky
> Of earth, and with what motion moved the clouds!

The 'what' is almost a question; questions and negatives play an important part in this style of extreme psychological truthfulness; they are not rhetorical or redundant; and he is never afraid of the flat prosy phrase if it seems to do the work. *Tintern Abbey* abounds in these negatives and qualifications. 'A sense sublime Of something far more deeply interfused'—more interfused than what? we may ask. 'If this Be but a vain belief' 'the motion of our human blood Almost suspended', and so on. Writing like this shows us that Wordsworth was not a philosopher in the sense of a man with a system of beliefs and attitudes to expound; nor was he a mystic, since the mystic usually knows where his insights are leading him and expects a graduated progress in the spiritual life, whereas Wordsworth's visions are often dim and fleeting ones; he is much more like a modern philosopher, a Ryle or a Sartre, starting off from a basis of complete scepticism and arguing carefully every step of the way until he can formulate a language which shall be an exact instrument for describing experience.

The famous banality of Wordsworth which measures the grave in *The Thorn* and finds it three feet long and two feet wide is all part of his fearless search for a diction which should bypass the pomposity of literature and take a sort of photograph or recording of experience itself, not just the scene but the emotion connected with the scene, the poetry which, as Wilfred Owen said, lies in the pity. At the time when he wrote the *Lyrical Ballads* he believed that instead of looking for his own way of saying the thing he might work dramatically; he might find in the incoherent, cliché-ridden talk of simple people the poetry of simple lives and have to heighten it only by the addition of metre. Hence *The Thorn*, a village tragedy of an unmarried mother which is supposed to be related by a long-winded, credulous village bore. The pathos shines out all the more through the account which, though half-comprehending, is close to the fact: it is the method of the great American realist novelists of the twentieth century, particularly of William Faulkner (a most Wordsworthian writer) and of Hemingway making the heroine of *Fiesta* characterize a moment of supreme moral choice in the words: 'It feels kind of good not to be a bitch'. And as in Caravaggio a sudden trick of the lighting throws an unexpected splendour among the brutal faces and the sordid interior, so the glory shines through the boredom of this account:

> At all times of the day and night
> This wretched Woman thither goes;
> And she is known to every star,
> And every wind that blows;
> And there beside the Thorn she sits
> When the blue day-light's in the skies,
> And when the whirlwind's on the hill,
> Or frosty air is keen and still,
> And to herself she cries,
> 'Oh misery! oh misery!
> Oh woe is me! oh misery!'

It is the achievements of the novelists in the century since Wordsworth which have made us most familiar with the sensitive use of the cliché; whatever the poets may do, every novelist follows Wordsworth's precepts and works with a selection of the language really used by men. To be sure, generations of pedants have rushed in to remind us that when he said this, in the Preface to *Lyrical Ballads*, he qualified it by adding 'in a state of vivid sensation'. But does vivid sensation make ordinary speech any less banal? I doubt it. Bogus fine writing betrays lack of emotional authenticity in many contemporary war books. Shakespeare convinces when he makes Lear in the moment of his agony say:

> Pray you undo this button, thank you, sir.

Wordsworth was right in his banalities, given the premises from which he started. Only the jog-trot metre and the inversions employed to contain ordinary conversation in short lines create an unhappy effect in some of the ballad poems. Perhaps he comes nearest to the modern novelist in *Animal Tranquility and Decay*, where the old man, completely resigned to what life shall send him, stretches hands to Faulkner's convict in *The Wild Palms* who endures so much:

> he was going many miles to take
> A last leave of his Son, a Mariner,
> Who from a sea-fight had been brought to Falmouth,
> And there was dying in an hospital.

Of course, it is impossible entirely to abolish or suppress the potentialities of poetic language and to take a photograph of experience, the thing as it really is, which will be able to provide the reader with the naked incident that has engaged the attention of the poet. This period of iconoclastic experiment taught Wordsworth to trust his own way of telling a story and not to imitate the speech of rustics; *Michael* has the bare dignity of his personal style and is far removed from the garrulousness of the ballads. Also the method of ultra-realism, as in the novelists and painters, ultimately creates its own type of rhetoric and becomes a mode of literature like any other. So Wordsworth developed a diction of his own, a diction we can recognize like a personal tone of voice, can admire and parody; but he kept it burnished as an instrument for exploring his consciousness; with it he continued to reach out beyond literature to talk of man and

> joy in widest commonalty spread

and he never let it turn in and feast upon itself. When his later poems disappoint through seeming too stiff and reliant on personification they are still almost painfully aware of a moral: the poem is pointing at something.

Among other characteristic features, the use of questions, of careful distinctions and of negative statements, the control of extremely simple statement which is nevertheless able to organize a wide range of emotional suggestion is perhaps the chief; it remains a dominant characteristic of his style long after the period of the experimental ballads. The single line in *Michael* which crystallizes the whole tragedy of the broken fortunes of the family symbolized by the unfinished sheep-cote has been famous ever since Arnold drew attention to it:

And never lifted up a single stone.

When Wordsworth visited France in 1802 he was shocked by what seemed to him the slavish adulation with which the French were proclaiming Napoleon consul for life, and he noticed the contrast with the festivals of liberty he had seen as a young man, travelling with his friend Jones, superficially similar but so different in the purity of their ideals. He wrote two sonnets, one beginning:

Festivals have I seen that were not names.

and the other:

Jones! as from Calais southward you and I.

The wealth of implication conveyed indirectly in these lines is tremendous, and in this context, just as he is able to make the most varied use of the verb 'to be', Wordsworth invests even the second commonest English surname with tones of passion and regret. It is misleading to call this quality simplicity since it is a method of deploying the whole emotional load of the poem at a certain point in its course and turning a flat statement into a very complex one.

After his power of emphatic statement, the weight and sonority of his language are most remarkable. No poet, even a Wordsworth, with his revolutionary programme for poetic languages can start from scratch; he must be reared within a particular literary tradition and as a young man learning to write must feel the influence of a dominant style. Wordsworth was educated on the poetry of the later eighteenth century, the school of Milton, which cultivated the linguistic habits of Latin poetry and used a number of words derived from it. On the whole it was an excellent discipline to grow up in: outside the experimental ballads his mature work, that of the creative phase as well as what he wrote in later years, is full of masterly use of the heavy Latinate word and phrase:

Thy friends are exultations, agonies.
And love, and Man's unconquerable mind.

                    I would chant the spousal verse
Of this great consummation.

Thou, thou, and all thy mates to keep
An incommunicable sleep.

(Notice the emphatic position in the line.)

                    Or the unimaginable touch of time.

Here in the sonorous, negative word the poet's imagination
points out its own limits as it stands in awe before the strange
decay which effaces the works of men. By such weightiness of
expression Wordsworth conveys the solemnity and moral
passion of his vision of life. But it is not a solemn earnestness of
personality imposing itself on reality; the gravity is in subjects
and the moral relations he is talking about and the heavy words
make us see them. The 'exultations' and 'agonies' of the sonnet
to Toussaint L'Ouverture, the liberator of Haiti, are not flowers
of rhetoric; with their substantive force they are a way of
saying that social and personal ideals have a life of their own and
are independent of circumstances: to allow the emotional key-
words to be abstract nouns is a form of poetic argument or
proof of this point.

His gifts of language are matched by great skill and variety
in the use of metre, though he does not possess the exquisite
sense of rhythm of a Spenser or a Milton; there is a northern
monotony of pitch about his work. His blank verse owes much
to the Miltonic tradition handed down through the didactic
poems of the eighteenth century which were written on everything from gardening to the faculties of the human mind; but
he endows it with a wholly individual character. The ballads,
however rustic, have life and speed, and often a haunting use of
the refrain. Wordsworth is one of the last poets to employ the

grand, choral form of the ode in irregular stanzas for a sublime subject (in *Intimations*). *Resolution and Independence* seems to be an entirely new kind of poem (though its metre was familiar in English poetry and had been used in the age before Wordsworth). It is a work of medium length dealing with a single incident in the poet's life which is described so as to provide a meditation on his hopes and fears, and a general expression of his sensibility. Shelley writes a poem of this kind in the *Lines written among the Euganean Hills*; Valéry's *Le Cimetière Marin* belongs to the genus and so do many of the poems of Yeats. Finally, in the sonnets we can see Wordsworth's artistic virtuosity admirably displayed on a miniature scale. In the stately, authoritative sonnet on public affairs he is the only successor of Milton; many fine miscellaneous sonnets, especially those in the later collections, are less well known.

The solidity and the hard outline which he displays in his verbal texture extends to the form of the whole poem. No poet has a finer sense of structure, of poetic shape. It has been well said that he is a classic among the romantics. His fondness for the sonnet shows that he rose to the challenge of a rigid, compressed pattern; but such a metrical skeleton can be artificial and restrictive to the thought of the poem. The structure of a Wordsworth poem is an organic form growing naturally out of the thought of the poet, related at each stage to the poetic emotion, and fusing together the metrical pattern and the whole complex of sounds and meanings. Terms like 'form', 'structure' and 'texture' which properly apply to the sort of object one can walk round and touch are no doubt sometimes abused when they are made to refer to works existing in time (the length of our reading) and lacking the special discipline of music. Wordsworth, however, in his shorter poems is peculiar in his faculty of creating an impression of almost architectural outline and solidity; this is the case, too, with the numerous poems in which the subject is a complex union of memory and present feeling, 'emotion recollected in tranquility'. In the four stanzas of *The Solitary Reaper* there is a natural movement from the girl seen in the field to the speculations of the traveller about the nature of her song and then back again to the singer before he loses sight of her as he goes over the hill; this movement coincides with a quiet beginning, a high point of emotion as the imagination eddies out to the furthest limits of speculation— deserts of Arabia and battles in old story—and then an equally quiet ending; having regard to this rise and fall we might describe the shape of the poem as a sort of pyramid. Then there are the poems like *Resolution and Independence* and the *Ode* where a mood of disquiet or regret described in the first part is balanced by an incident or a train of thought in the later part which seems to provide a solution to the problem; there is a firm structure of poetic argument, which is not the same as logical argument since it depends not on verbal proof but on the convincing presentation of emotional states. In other poems the predominant emotion is strongly focused by the stress thrown on some particular incident, object or person: the untouched pile of stones in *Michael* (recalling the mind to the other eminence of the poem, the busy cottage at the head of the valley with its lamp blazing out to the neighbourhood late at night), the angelically gentle doe in *The White Doe*, symbol of Emily's resignation, and the gaunt, silhouetted figures of the solitaries in many poems.

Wordsworth is, then, a great artist, not a thinker thinking in verse and a poet only fitfully or by accident. But he shows us a literary art which can palpably transmit the very form and pressure of a moral vision of life. He gives, if not a philosophy, then wisdom; a gift not always available even from philosophers. He believes that the harmony he detects in the goings-on of the universe is somehow ultimately reflected in the life of man; we can finally become reconciled to evil and pain if we contemplate them aright. This is an attitude that can be held on different grounds; it may express only the most selfish defence of the *status quo*, the shallow optimism of Dr. Pangloss saying that all is for the best in the best of all possible worlds. Wordsworth, however, never glosses over the reality of suffering: his many revisions of the ending to the story of the bereaved Margaret (*The Ruined Cottage*) illustrate his preoccupation with this problem, and even before he substituted an overtly Christian solution he obviously thought that some sort of consolation was to be found. He may seem stoically bleak, but never priggish. In his humble people, solitaries and heroes of duty, he praises the regular beauty of common life, the ordinary round of daily work, begetting, bringing up children and dying. This is perhaps where modern taste with its preference for a special, high-flying extraordinary conception of the good life is most liable to be irritated with him, even when his poetic greatness has been accepted. It can tolerate a respectable, disciplined man *or* a passionate free spirit; what shocks all its preconceptions—its newfangled idea of decorum—is the spectacle of the latter growing into the former; the conscious restraint of passion in order to attain permanence and continuity. The solitary is not an outsider. Yet this quality is the most important Wordsworth has to offer the modern world. In the naked isolation of sensibility from which he builds up his vision of the world he is the prototype of all modern writers. But he moves from his isolation to an understanding of the brotherhood of man:

> by words
> Which speak of nothing more than what we are,
> Would I arouse the sensual from their sleep
> Of Death, and win the vacant and the vain
> To noble raptures.

SELECTED POEMS

EXTRACTS FROM
THE PRELUDE

Fair Seed-time

(*Book I.* 305–489)

Fair seed-time had my soul, and I grew up　　　　305
Fostered alike by beauty and by fear;
Much favoured in my birthplace, and no less
In that beloved Vale to which, erelong,
I was transplanted. Well I call to mind
('Twas at an early age, ere I had seen　　　　310
Nine summers) when upon the mountain slope
The frost and breath of frosty wind had snapped
The last autumnal crocus, 'twas my joy
To wander half the night among the Cliffs
And the smooth Hollows, where the woodcocks ran　315
Along the open turf. In thought and wish
That time, my shoulder all with springes hung,
I was a fell destroyer. On the heights
Scudding away from snare to snare, I plied
My anxious visitation, hurrying on,　　　　320
Still hurrying, hurrying onward; moon and stars
Were shining o'er my head; I was alone,
And seem'd to be a trouble to the peace
That was among them. Sometimes it befel
In these night-wanderings, that a strong desire　325
O'erpowered my better reason, and the bird
Which was the captive of another's toils

I

Became my prey; and, when the deed was done
I heard among the solitary hills
Low breathings coming after me, and sounds   330
Of undistinguishable motion, steps
Almost as silent as the turf they trod.
Nor less in springtime when on southern banks
The shining sun had from his knot of leaves
Decoy'd the primrose flower, and when the Vales   335
And woods were warm, was I a plunderer then
In the high places, on the lonesome peaks
Where'er among the mountains and the winds,
The Mother Bird had built her lodge. Though mean
My object, and inglorious, yet the end   340
Was not ignoble. Oh! when I have hung
Above the raven's nest, by knots of grass
And half-inch fissures in the slippery rock
But ill sustain'd, and almost, as it seemed
Suspended by the blast which blew amain,   345
Shouldering the naked crag; Oh! at that time,
While on the perilous ridge I hung alone,
With what strange utterance did the loud dry wind
Blow through my ears! the sky seem'd not a sky
Of earth, and with what motion moved the clouds!   350

　　The mind of Man is fram'd even like the breath
And harmony of music. There is a dark
Invisible workmanship that reconciles
Discordant elements, and makes them move
In one society. Ah me! that all   355
The terrors, all the early miseries
Regrets, vexations, lassitudes, that all
The thoughts and feelings which have been infus'd
Into my mind, should ever have made up
The calm existence that is mine when I   360

Am worthy of myself! Praise to the end!
Thanks likewise for the means! But I believe
That Nature, oftentimes, when she would frame
A favoured Being, from his earliest dawn
Of infancy doth open up the clouds,   365
As at the touch of lightning, seeking him
With gentlest visitation; not the less,
Though haply aiming at the self-same end,
Does it delight her sometimes to employ
Severer interventions, ministry   370
More palpable, and so she dealt with me.

    One evening (surely I was led by her)
I went alone into a Shepherd's Boat
A Skiff that to a Willow tree was tied
Within a rocky Cave, its usual home.   375
'Twas by the shores of Patterdale, a Vale
Wherein I was a Stranger, thither come
A School-boy Traveller, at the Holidays.
Forth rambled from the Village Inn alone
No sooner had I sight of this small Skiff,   380
Discover'd thus by unexpected chance,
Than I unloosed her tether and embarked.
The moon was up, the Lake was shining clear
Among the hoary mountains; from the Shore
I pushed, and struck the oars and struck again   385
In cadence, and my little Boat mov'd on
Even like a Man who walks with stately step
Though bent on speed. It was an act of stealth
And troubled pleasure; not without the voice
Of mountain-echoes did my Boat move on,   390
Leaving behind her still on either side
Small circles glittering idly in the moon,
Until they melted all into one track

3

Of sparkling light. A rocky Steep uprose
Above the Cavern of the Willow tree   395
And now, as suited one who proudly row'd
With his best skill, I fix'd a steady view
Upon the top of that same craggy ridge,
The bound of the horizon, for behind
Was nothing but the stars and the grey sky.   400
She was an elfin Pinnace; lustily
I dipped my oars into the silent Lake,
And, as I rose upon the stroke, my Boat
Went heaving through the water, like a Swan;
When from behind that craggy Steep, till then   405
The bound of the horizon, a huge Cliff,
As if with voluntary power instinct,
Upreared its head. I struck, and struck again,
And growing still in stature, the huge Cliff
Rose up between me and the stars, and still,   410
With measur'd motion, like a living thing,
Strode after me. With trembling hands I turned,
And through the silent water stole my way
Back to the Cavern of the Willow tree.
There, in her mooring-place, I left my Bark,   415
And, through the meadows homeward went, with grave
And serious thoughts; and after I had seen
That spectacle, for many days, my brain
Worked with a dim and undetermin'd sense
Of unknown modes of being; in my thoughts   420
There was a darkness, call it solitude,
Or blank desertion, no familiar shapes
Of hourly objects, images of trees
Of sea or sky, no colours of green fields;
But huge and mighty Forms that do not live   425
Like living men mov'd slowly through the mind
By day and were the trouble of my dreams.

4

Wisdom and Spirit of the universe!
Thou Soul that art the eternity of thought!
That giv'st to forms and images a breath   430
And everlasting motion! not in vain,
By day or star-light thus from my first dawn
Of Childhood didst Thou intertwine for me
The passions that build up our human Soul,
Not with the mean and vulgar works of Man,   435
But with high objects, with enduring things,
With life and nature, purifying thus
The elements of feeling and of thought,
And sanctifying, by such discipline,
Both pain and fear, until we recognize   440
A grandeur in the beatings of the heart.

Nor was this fellowship vouchsafed to me
With stinted kindness. In November days,
When vapours, rolling down the valleys, made
A lonely scene more lonesome; among woods   445
At noon, and 'mid the calm of summer nights,
When, by the margin of the trembling Lake,
Beneath the gloomy hills I homeward went
In solitude, such intercourse was mine;
'Twas mine among the fields both day and night,   450
And by the waters all the summer long.

And in the frosty season, when the sun
Was set, and visible for many a mile
The cottage windows through the twilight blaz'd,
I heeded not the summons:—happy time   455
It was, indeed, for all of us; to me
It was a time of rapture: clear and loud
The village clock tolled six; I wheel'd about,
Proud and exulting, like an untired horse,

That cares not for his home.—All shod with steel,   460
We hissed along the polished ice, in games
Confederate, imitative of the chace
And woodland pleasures, the resounding horn,
The Pack loud bellowing, and the hunted hare.
So through the darkness and the cold we flew,   465
And not a voice was idle; with the din,
Meanwhile, the precipices rang aloud,
The leafless trees, and every icy crag
Tinkled like iron, while the distant hills
Into the tumult sent an alien sound   470
Of melancholy, not unnoticed, while the stars,
Eastward, were sparkling clear, and in the west
The orange sky of evening died away.

    Not seldom from the uproar I retired
Into a silent bay, or sportively   475
Glanced sideway, leaving the tumultuous throng,
To cut across the image of a star
That gleam'd upon the ice: and oftentimes
When we had given our bodies to the wind,
And all the shadowy banks, on either side,   480
Came sweeping through the darkness, spinning still
The rapid line of motion; then at once
Have I, reclining back upon my heels,
Stopp'd short, yet still the solitary Cliffs
Wheeled by me, even as if the earth had roll'd   485
With visible motion her diurnal round;
Behind me did they stretch in solemn train
Feebler and feebler, and I stood and watch'd
Till all was tranquil as a dreamless sleep.

Poetic Dedication

(Book IV. 316–345)

In a throng,

A festal company of Maids and Youths,
Old Men, and Matrons staid, promiscuous rout,
A medley of all tempers, I had pass'd
The night in dancing, gaiety and mirth;   320
With din of instruments, and shuffling feet,
And glancing forms, and tapers glittering,
And unaim'd prattle flying up and down,
Spirits upon the stretch, and here and there
Slight shocks of young love-liking interspers'd   325
That mounted up like joy into the head,
And tingled through the veins. Ere we retired,
The cock had crow'd, the sky was bright with day.
Two miles I had to walk along the fields
Before I reached my home. Magnificent   330
The morning was, in memorable pomp,
More glorious than I ever had beheld.
The Sea was laughing at a distance; all
The solid Mountains were as bright as clouds,
Grain-tinctured, drench'd in empyrean light;   335
And, in the meadows and the lower grounds,
Was all the sweetness of a common dawn,
Dews, vapours, and the melody of birds,
And Labourers going forth into the fields.
—Ah! need I say, dear Friend, that to the brim   340
My heart was full; I made no vows, but vows
Were then made for me; bond unknown to me

7

Was given, that I should be, else sinning greatly,
A dedicated Spirit. On I walk'd
In blessedness, which even yet remains.   345

'There Was a Boy'

(Book V. 389–413)

There was a Boy, ye knew him well, ye Cliffs
And Islands of Winander! many a time   390
At evening, when the stars had just begun
To move along the edges of the hills,
Rising or setting, would he stand alone
Beneath the trees, or by the glimmering Lake,
And there, with fingers interwoven, both hands   395
Press'd closely, palm to palm, and to his mouth
Uplifted, he, as through an instrument,
Blew mimic hootings to the silent owls
That they might answer him.—And they would shout
Across the watery Vale, and shout again,   400
Responsive to his call, with quivering peals,
And long halloos, and screams, and echoes loud
Redoubled and redoubled; concourse wild
Of mirth and jocund din! And when it chanced
That pauses of deep silence mock'd his skill,   405
Then sometimes, in that silence, while he hung
Listening, a gentle shock of mild surprize
Has carried far into his heart the voice
Of mountain torrents; or the visible scene
Would enter unawares into his mind   410
With all its solemn imagery, its rocks,
Its woods, and that uncertain Heaven, received
Into the bosom of the steady Lake.

The Nature of Poetry

(Book V. 516–557)

A gracious Spirit o'er this earth presides,
And o'er the heart of man: invisibly
It comes, directing those to works of love
Who care not, know not, think not what they do:
The Tales that charm away the wakeful night   520
In Araby, Romances, Legends, penn'd
For solace, by the light of monkish Lamps;
Fictions for Ladies, of their Love, devis'd
By youthful Squires; adventures endless, spun
By the dismantled Warrior in old age,   525
Out of the bowels of those very thoughts
In which his youth did first extravagate,
These spread like day, and something in the shape
Of these, will live till man shall be no more.
Dumb yearnings, hidden appetites are ours,   530
And they must have their food: our childhood sits,
Our simple childhood sits upon a throne
That hath more power than all the elements.
I guess not what this tells of Being past,
Nor what it augurs of the life to come;   535
But so it is; and in that dubious hour,
That twilight when we first begin to see
This dawning earth, to recognize, expect
And in the long probation that ensues,
The time of trial, ere we learn to live   540
In reconcilement with our stinted powers,
To endure this state of meagre vassalage;

9

Unwilling to forego, confess, submit,
Uneasy and unsettled, yoke-fellows
To custom, mettlesome, and not yet tam'd   545
And humbled down, oh! then we feel, we feel,
We know when we have Friends. Ye dreamers, then,
Forgers of lawless tales! we bless you then,
Impostors, drivellers, dotards, as the ape
Philosophy will call you: then we feel   550
With what, and how great might ye are in league,
Who make our wish our power, our thought a deed,
An empire, a possession; Ye whom Time
And Seasons serve; all Faculties; to whom
Earth crouches, th' elements are potter's clay,   555
Space like a Heaven fill'd up with Northern lights;
Here, nowhere, there, and everywhere at once.

Visionary Power

(Book V. 608–629)

Here must I pause: this only will I add,
From heart-experience, and in humblest sense
Of modesty, that he, who, in his youth   610
A wanderer among the woods and fields,
With living Nature hath been intimate,
Not only in that raw unpractis'd time
Is stirred to ecstasy, as others are,
By glittering verse; but, he doth furthermore,   615
In measure only dealt out to himself,
Receive enduring touches of deep joy
From the great Nature that exists in works
Of mighty Poets. Visionary Power

Attends upon the motions of the winds   620
Embodied in the mystery of words.
There darkness makes abode, and all the host
Of shadowy things do work their changes there,
As in a mansion like their proper home;
Even forms and substances are circumfused   625
By that transparent veil with light divine;
And through the turnings intricate of Verse,
Present themselves as objects recogniz'd,
In flashes, and with a glory scarce their own.

Crossing the Alps

(Book VI. 525–572)

Imagination! lifting up itself   525
Before the eye and progress of my Song
Like an unfather'd vapour; here that Power,
In all the might of its endowments, came
Athwart me; I was lost as in a cloud,
Halted, without a struggle to break through.   530
And now recovering, to my Soul I say
I recognize thy glory; in such strength
Of usurpation, in such visitings
Of awful promise, when the light of sense
Goes out in flashes that have shewn to us   535
The invisible world, doth Greatness make abode,
There harbours whether we be young or old.
Our destiny, our nature, and our home
Is with infinitude, and only there;
With hope it is, hope that can never die,   540
Effort, and expectation, and desire,

11

And something evermore about to be.
The mind beneath such banners militant
Thinks not of spoils or trophies, nor of aught
That may attest its prowess, blest in thoughts   545
That are their own perfection and reward,
Strong in itself, and in the access of joy
Which hides it like the overflowing Nile.

     The dull and heavy slackening that ensued
Upon those tidings by the Peasant given   550
Was soon dislodged; downwards we hurried fast,
And enter'd with the road which we had miss'd
Into a narrow chasm; the brook and road
Were fellow-travellers in this gloomy Pass,
And with them did we journey several hours   555
At a slow step. The immeasurable height
Of woods decaying, never to be decay'd,
The stationary blasts of water-falls,
And every where along the hollow rent
Winds thwarting winds, bewilder'd and forlorn,   560
The torrents shooting from the clear blue sky,
The rocks that mutter'd close upon our ears.
Black drizzling crags that spake by the way-side
As if a voice were in them, the sick sight
And giddy prospect of the raving stream,   565
The unfetter'd clouds, and region of the Heavens,
Tumult and peace, the darkness and the light
Were all like workings of one mind, the features
Of the same face, blossoms upon one tree,
Characters of the great Apocalypse,   570
The types and symbols of Eternity,
Of first and last, and midst, and without end.

London Images

(Book VII. 594–740)

How often in the overflowing Streets,
Have I gone forward with the Crowd, and said   595
Unto myself, the face of every one
That passes by me is a mystery.
Thus have I look'd, nor ceas'd to look, oppress'd
By thoughts of what, and whither, when and how
Until the shapes before my eyes became   600
A second-sight procession, such as glides
Over still mountains, or appears in dreams;
And all the ballast of familiar life,
The present, and the past; hope, fear; all stays,
All laws of acting, thinking, speaking man   605
Went from me, neither knowing me, nor known.
And once, far-travell'd in such mood, beyond
The reach of common indications, lost
Amid the moving pageant, 'twas my chance
Abruptly to be smitten with the view   610
Of a blind Beggar, who, with upright face,
Stood propp'd against a Wall, upon his Chest
Wearing a written paper, to explain
The story of the Man, and who he was.
My mind did at this spectacle turn round   615
As with the might of waters, and it seemed
To me that in this Label was a type,
Or emblem, of the utmost that we know,
Both of ourselves and of the universe;
And, on the shape of the unmoving man,   620

13

His fixèd face and sightless eyes, I look'd
As if admonish'd from another world.
    Though rear'd upon the base of outward things,
These, chiefly, are such structures as the mind
Builds for itself. Scenes different there are,   625
Full-form'd, which take, with small internal help,
Possession of the faculties; the peace
Of night, for instance, the solemnity
Of nature's intermediate hours of rest,
When the great tide of human life stands still,   630
The business of the day to come unborn,
Of that gone by, lock'd up as in the grave;
The calmness, beauty, of the spectacle,
Sky, stillness, moonshine, empty streets, and sounds
Unfrequent as in desarts; at late hours   635
Of winter evenings when unwholesome rains
Are falling hard, with people yet astir,
The feeble salutation from the voice
Of some unhappy Woman, now and then
Heard as we pass; when no one looks about,   640
Nothing is listen'd to. But these, I fear,
Are falsely catalogu'd, things that are, are not,
Even as we give them welcome, or assist,
Are prompt, or are remiss. What say you then,
To times, when half the City shall break out   645
Full of one passion, vengeance, rage, or fear,
To executions, to a Street on fire,
Mobs, riots, or rejoicings? From these sights
Take one, an annual Festival, the Fair
Holden where Martyrs suffer'd in past time,   650
And named of Saint Bartholomew; there see
A work that's finish'd to our hands, that lays,
If any spectacle on earth can do,
The whole creative powers of man asleep!

14

For once the Muse's help will we implore,   655
And she shall lodge us, wafted on her wings,
Above the press and danger of the Crowd,
Upon some Showman's platform; what a hell
For eyes and ears! what anarchy and din
Barbarian and infernal! 'tis a dream,   660
Monstrous in colour, motion, shape, sight, sound.
Below, the open space, through every nook
Of the wide area, twinkles, is alive
With heads; the midway region and above
Is throng'd with staring pictures, and huge scrolls,   665
Dumb proclamations of the prodigies;
And chattering monkeys dangling from their poles,
And children whirling in their roundabouts;
With those that stretch the neck, and strain the eyes.
And crack the voice in rivalship, the crowd   670
Inviting; with buffoons against buffoons
Grimacing, writhing, screaming; him who grinds
The hurdy-gurdy, at the fiddle weaves;
Rattles the salt-box, thumps the kettle-drum,
And him who at the trumpet puffs his cheeks,   675
The silver-collar'd Negro with his timbrel,
Equestrians, Tumblers, Women, Girls, and Boys,
Blue-breech'd, pink-vested, and with towering plumes.
—All moveables of wonder from all parts,
Are here, Albinos, painted Indians, Dwarfs,   680
The Horse of Knowledge, and the learned Pig,
The Stone-eater, the Man that swallows fire,
Giants, Ventriloquists, the Invisible Girl,
The Bust that speaks, and moves its goggling eyes,
The Wax-work, Clock-work, all the marvellous craft   685
Of modern Merlins, wild Beasts, Puppet-shows,
All out-o'-the-way, far-fetch'd, perverted things,
All freaks of Nature, all Promethean thoughts

Of Man; his dulness, madness, and their feats,
All jumbled up together to make up   690
This Parliament of Monsters. Tents and Booths
Meanwhile, as if the whole were one vast Mill,
Are vomiting, receiving, on all sides,
Men, Women, three-years' Children, Babes in arms.

    Oh, blank confusion! and a type not false   695
Of what the mighty City is itself
To all except a Straggler here and there,
To the whole Swarm of its inhabitants;
An undistinguishable world to men,
The slaves unrespited of low pursuits,   700
Living amid the same perpetual flow
Of trivial objects, melted and reduced
To one identity, by differences
That have no law, no meaning, and no end;
Oppression under which even highest minds   705
Must labour, whence the strongest are not free;
But though the picture weary out the eye,
By nature an unmanageable sight,
It is not wholly so to him who looks
In steadiness, who hath among least things   710
An under-sense of greatest; sees the parts
As parts, but with a feeling of the whole.
This, of all acquisitions first, awaits
On sundry and most widely different modes
Of education; nor with least delight   715
On that through which I pass'd. Attention comes,
And comprehensiveness and memory,
From early converse with the works of God
Among all regions; chiefly where appear
Most obviously simplicity and power.   720
By influence habitual to the mind

The mountain's outline and its steady form
Gives a pure grandeur, and its presence shapes
The measure and the prospect of the soul
To majesty; such virtue have the forms   725
Perennial of the ancient hills; nor less
The changeful language of their countenances
Gives movement to the thoughts, and multitude,
With order and relation. This, if still,
As hitherto, with freedom I may speak,   730
And the same perfect openness of mind,
Not violating any just restraint,
As I would hope, of real modesty,
This did I feel in that vast receptacle.
The Spirit of Nature was upon me here;   735
The Soul of Beauty and enduring life
Was present as a habit, and diffused,
Through meagre lines and colours, and the press
Of self-destroying, transitory things
Composure and ennobling Harmony.   740

Love of Nature and Love of Man

(Book VIII. 119–310)

                    Beauteous the domain
Where to the sense of beauty first my heart   120
Was open'd, tract more exquisitely fair
Than is that Paradise of ten thousand Trees,
Or Gehol's famous Gardens, in a Clime
Chosen from widest empire, for delight
Of the Tartarian Dynasty composed;   125
(Beyond that mighty Wall, not fabulous,
China's stupendous mound!) by patient skill

Of myriads, and boon Nature's lavish help;
Scene link'd to scene, an evergrowing change,
Soft, grand, or gay! with Palaces and Domes   130
Of Pleasure spangled over, shady Dells
For Eastern Monasteries, sunny Mounds
With Temples crested, Bridges, Gondolas,
Rocks, Dens, and Groves of foliage taught to melt
Into each other their obsequious hues   135
Going and gone again, in subtile chace,
Too fine to be pursued; or standing forth
In no discordant opposition, strong
And gorgeous as the colours side by side
Bedded among rich plumes of Tropic Birds;   140
And mountains over all embracing all;
And all the landscape endlessly enrich'd
With waters running, falling, or asleep.

But lovelier far than this the Paradise
Where I was reared; in Nature's primitive gifts   145
Favor'd no less, and more to every sense
Delicious, seeing that the sun and sky,
The elements and seasons in their change
Do find their dearest Fellow-labourer there,
The heart of Man, a district on all sides   150
The fragrance breathing of humanity,
Man free, man working for himself, with choice
Of time, and place, and object; by his wants,
His comforts, native occupations, cares,
Conducted on to individual ends   155
Or social, and still followed by a train
Unwoo'd, unthought-of even, simplicity,
And beauty, and inevitable grace.

Yea, doubtless, at an age when but a glimpse

Of those resplendent Gardens, with their frame   160
Imperial, and elaborate ornaments,
Would to a child be transport over-great,
When but a half-hour's roam through such a place
Would leave behind a dance of images
That shall break in upon his sleep for weeks;   165
Even then the common haunts of the green earth,
With the ordinary human interests
Which they embosom, all without regard
As both may seem, are fastening on the heart
Insensibly, each with the other's help,   170
So that we love, not knowing that we love,
And feel, not knowing whence our feeling comes.

   Such league have these two principles of joy
In our affections. I have singled out
Some moments, the earliest that I could, in which   175
Their several currents blended into one,
Weak yet, and gathering imperceptibly,
Flow'd in by gushes. My first human love,
As hath been mentioned, did incline to those
Whose occupations and concerns were most   180
Illustrated by Nature and adorn'd,
And Shepherds were the men who pleas'd me first.
Not such as in Arcadian Fastnesses
Sequester'd, handed down among themselves,
So ancient Poets sing, the golden Age;   185
Nor such, a second Race, allied to these,
As Shakespeare in the Wood of Arden placed
Where Phoebe sighed for the false Ganymede,
Or there where Florizel and Perdita
Together danc'd, Queen of the Feast and King;   190
Nor such as Spenser fabled. True it is,
That I heard (what he perhaps had seen)

Of maids at sunrise bringing in from far
Their May-bush, and along the Streets, in flocks,
Parading with a Song of taunting Rhymes,   195
Aim'd at the Laggards slumbering within doors;
Had also heard, from those who yet remembered,
Tales of the May-pole Dance, and flowers that decked
The Posts and the Kirk-pillars, and of Youths,
That each one with his Maid, at break of day,   200
By annual custom issued forth in troops,
To drink the waters of some favorite well,
And hang it round with Garlands. This, alas!
Was but a dream; the times had scatter'd all
These lighter graces, and the rural custom   205
And manners which it was my chance to see
In childhood were severe and unadorn'd,
The unluxuriant produce of a life
Intent on little but substantial needs,
Yet beautiful, and beauty that was felt.   210
But images of danger and distress,
And suffering among awful Powers, and Forms;
Of this I heard and saw enough to make
The imagination restless; nor was free
Myself from frequent perils; nor were tales   215
Wanting, the tragedies of former times,
Of hazards and escapes, which in my walks
I carried with me among crags and woods
And mountains; and of these may here be told
One, as recorded by my Household Dame.   220

    At the first falling of autumnal snow
A Shepherd and his Son one day went forth
(Thus did the Matron's Tale begin) to seek
A Straggler of their Flock. They both had rang'd
Upon this service the preceding day   225

All over their own pastures and beyond,
And now, at sun-rise sallying out again
Renew'd their search begun where from Dove Crag,
Ill home for bird so gentle, they looked down
On Deep-dale Head, and Brothers-water, named   230
From those two Brothers that were drowned therein.
Thence, northward, having pass'd by Arthur's Seat,
To Fairfield's highest summit; on the right
Leaving St. Sunday's Pike, to Grisedale Tarn
They shot, and over that cloud-loving Hill,   235
Seat Sandal, a fond lover of the clouds;
Thence up Helvellyn, a superior Mount
With prospect underneath of Striding-Edge,
And Grisedale's houseless Vale, along the brink
Of Russet Cove, and those two other Coves,   240
Huge skeletons of crags, which from the trunk
Of old Helvellyn spread their arms abroad,
And make a stormy harbour for the winds.
Far went those Shepherds in their devious quest,
From mountain ridges peeping as they passed   245
Down into every Glen; at length the Boy
Said, 'Father, with your leave I will go back,
And range the ground which we have search'd before.'
So speaking, southward down the hill the Lad
Sprang like a gust of wind, crying aloud   250
'I know where I shall find him.' 'For take note,
Said here my grey-haired Dame, that tho' the storm
Drive one of these poor Creatures miles and miles,
If he can crawl he will return again
To his own hills, the spots where, when a Lamb,   255
He learn'd to pasture at his Mother's side.'
After so long a labour, suddenly
Bethinking him of this, the Boy
Pursued his way towards a brook whose course

Was through that unfenced tract of mountain-ground   260
Which to his Father's little Farm belong'd,
The home and ancient Birth-right of their Flock.
Down the deep channel of the Stream he went,
Prying through every nook; meanwhile the rain
Began to fall upon the mountain tops,   265
Thick storm and heavy which for three hours' space
Abated not; and all that time the Boy
Was busy in his search until at length
He spied the Sheep upon a plot of grass,
An Island in the Brook. It was a Place   270
Remote and deep, piled round with rocks where foot
Of man or beast was seldom used to tread;
But now, when everywhere the summer grass
Had fail'd, this one Adventurer, hunger-press'd,
Had left his Fellows, and made his way alone   275
To the green plot of pasture in the Brook.
Before the Boy knew well what he had seen
He leapt upon the Island with proud heart
And with a Prophet's joy. Immediately
The Sheep sprang forward to the further Shore   280
And was borne headlong by the roaring flood.
At this the Boy look'd round him, and his heart
Fainted with fear; thrice did he turn his face
To either brink; nor could he summon up
The courage that was needful to leap back   285
Cross the tempestuous torrent; so he stood,
A Prisoner on the Island, not without
More than one thought of death and his last hour.
Meanwhile the Father had return'd alone
To his own house; and now at the approach   290
Of evening he went forth to meet his Son,
Conjecturing vainly for what cause the Boy
Had stay'd so long. The Shepherd took his way

Up his own mountain grounds, where, as he walk'd
Along the Steep that overhung the Brook,   295
He seemed to hear a voice, which was again
Repeated, like the whistling of a kite.
At this, not knowing why, as oftentimes
Long afterwards he has been heard to say,
Down to the Brook he went, and track'd its course   300
Upwards among the o'erhanging rocks, nor thus
Had he gone far, ere he espied the Boy
Where on that little plot of ground he stood
Right in the middle of the roaring Stream,
Now stronger every moment and more fierce.   305
The sight was such as no one could have seen
Without distress and fear. The Shepherd heard
The outcry of his Son, he stretch'd his Staff
Towards him, bade him leap, which word scarce said
The Boy was safe within his Father's arms.   310

The French Revolution

(Book X. 690–728)

O pleasant exercise of hope and joy!   690
For great were the auxiliars which then stood
Upon our side, we who were strong in love;
Bliss was it in that dawn to be alive,
But to be young was very heaven; O times,
In which the meagre, stale, forbidding ways   695
Of custom, law, and statute took at once
The attraction of a Country in Romance;
When Reason seem'd the most to assert her rights
When most intent on making of herself

23

A prime Enchanter to assist the work,   700
Which then was going forwards in her name.
Not favour'd spots alone, but the whole earth
The beauty wore of promise, that which sets,
To take an image which was felt, no doubt,
Among the bowers of paradise itself,   705
The budding rose above the rose full blown.
What temper at the prospect did not wake
To happiness unthought of? The inert
Were rouz'd, and lively natures rapt away:
They who had fed their childhood upon dreams,   710
The Play-fellows of Fancy, who had made
All powers of swiftness, subtlety, and strength
Their ministers, used to stir in lordly wise
Among the grandest objects of the sense,
And deal with whatsoever they found there   715
As if they had within some lurking right
To wield it; they too, who, of gentle mood
Had watch'd all gentle motions, and to these
Had fitted their own thoughts, schemers more mild,
And in the region of their peaceful selves,   720
Did now find helpers to their hearts' desire,
And stuff at hand, plastic as they could wish,
Were called upon to exercise their skill,
Not in Utopia, subterraneous Fields,
Or some secreted Island, Heaven knows where,   725
But in the very world which is the world
Of all of us, the place in which, in the end,
We find our happiness, or not at all.

Time Regained

(Book XI. 258–389)

There are in our existence spots of time,
Which with distinct pre-eminence retain
A vivifying Virtue, whence, depress'd   260
By false opinion and contentious thought,
Or aught of heavier or more deadly weight,
In trivial occupations, and the round
Of ordinary intercourse, our minds
Are nourished and invisibly repair'd,   265
A virtue by which pleasure is enhanced
That penetrates, enables us to mount
When high, more high, and lifts us up when fallen
This efficacious spirit chiefly lurks
Among those passages of life in which   270
We have had deepest feeling that the mind
Is lord and master, and that outward sense
Is but the obedient servant of her will.
Such moments worthy of all gratitude,
Are scatter'd everywhere, taking their date   275
From our first childhood: in our childhood even
Perhaps are most conspicuous. Life with me,
As far as memory can look back, is full
Of this beneficent influence. At a time
When scarcely (I was then not six years old)   280
My hand could hold a bridle, with proud hopes
I mounted, and we rode towards the hills:
We were a pair of horsemen; honest James

Was with me, my encourager and guide.
We had not travelled long, ere some mischance   285
Disjoin'd me from my Comrade, and, through fear
Dismounting, down the rough and stony Moor
I led my Horse, and stumbling on, at length
Came to a bottom, where in former times
A Murderer had been hung in iron chains.   290
The Gibbet-mast was moulder'd down, the bones
And iron case were gone; but on the turf,
Hard by, soon after that fell deed was wrought
Some unknown hand had carved the Murderer's name.
The monumental writing was engraven   295
In times long past, and still, from year to year,
By superstition of the neighbourhood,
The grass is clear'd away; and to this hour
The letters are all fresh and visible.
Faltering, and ignorant where I was, at length   300
I chanced to espy those characters inscribed
On the green sod: forthwith I left the spot
And, reascending the bare Common, saw
A naked Pool that lay beneath the hills,
The Beacon on the summit, and more near,   305
A Girl who bore a Pitcher on her head
And seem'd with difficult steps to force her way
Against the blowing wind. It was, in truth,
An ordinary sight; but I should need
Colours and words that are unknown to man   310
To paint the visionary dreariness
Which, while I looked all round for my lost guide,
Did at that time invest the naked Pool,
The Beacon on the lonely Eminence,
The Woman, and her garments vex'd and toss'd   315
By the strong wind. When, in a blessed season
With those two dear Ones, to my heart so dear,

When in the blessed time of early love,
Long afterwards, I roam'd about
In daily presence of this very scene,   320
Upon the naked pool and dreary crags,
And on the melancholy Beacon, fell
The spirit of pleasure and youth's golden gleam;
And think ye not with radiance more divine
From these remembrances, and from the power   325
They left behind? So feeling comes in aid
Of feeling, and diversity of strength
Attends us, if but once we have been strong.
Oh! mystery of Man, from what a depth
Proceed thy honours! I am lost, but see   330
In simple childhood something of the base
On which thy greatness stands, but this I feel,
That from thyself it is that thou must give,
Else never canst receive. The days gone by
Come back upon me from the dawn almost   335
Of life: the hiding-places of my power
Seem open; I approach, and then they close;
I see by glimpses now; when age comes on,
May scarcely see at all, and I would give,
While yet we may, as far as words can give,   340
A substance and a life to what I feel:
I would enshrine the spirit of the past
For future restoration. Yet another
Of these to me affecting incidents
With which we will conclude.   345
                    One Christmas-time,
The day before the holidays began,
Feverish and tired, and restless, I went forth
Into the fields, impatient for the sight
Of those two Horses which should bear us home;
My Brothers and myself. There was a crag,   350

An Eminence, which from the meeting-point
Of two highways ascending, overlook'd
At least a long half-mile of those two roads,
By each of which the expected Steeds might come,
The choice uncertain. Thither I repaired   355
Up to the highest summit; 'twas a day
Stormy, and rough, and wild, and on the grass
I sate, half-shelter'd by a naked wall;
Upon my right hand was a single sheep,
A whistling hawthorn on my left, and there,   360
With those companions at my side, I watch'd,
Straining my eyes intensely, as the mist
Gave intermitting prospect of the wood
And plain beneath. Ere I to School return'd
That dreary time, ere I had been ten days   365
A dweller in my Father's House, he died,
And I and my two Brothers, Orphans then,
Followed his Body to the Grave. The event
With all the sorrow which it brought appear'd
A chastisement; and when I call'd to mind   370
That day so lately passed, when from the crag
I looked in such anxiety of hope,
With trite reflections of morality,
Yet in the deepest passion, I bow'd low
To God, who thus corrected my desires;   375
And afterwards, the wind and sleety rain
And all the business of the elements,
The single sheep, and the one blasted tree,
And the bleak music of that old stone wall,
The noise of wood and water, and the mist   380
Which on the line of each of those two Roads
Advanced in such indisputable shapes,
All these were spectacles and sounds to which
I often would repair and thence would drink,

As at a fountain; and I do not doubt
That in this later time, when storm and rain
Beat on my roof at midnight, or by day
When I am in the woods, unknown to me
The workings of my spirit thence are brought.

Prospectus to *The Recluse*

On Man, on Nature, and on Human Life,
Musing in solitude, I oft perceive
Fair trains of imagery before me rise,
Accompanied by feelings of delight
Pure, or with no unpleasing sadness mixed;   5
And I am conscious of affecting thoughts
And dear remembrances, whose presence soothes
Or elevates the Mind, intent to weigh
The good and evil of our mortal state.
—To these emotions, whencesoe'er they come,   10
Whether from breath of outward circumstance,
Or from the Soul—an impulse to herself—
I would give utterance in numerous verse.
Of Truth, of Grandeur, Beauty, Love, and Hope,
And melancholy Fear subdued by Faith;   15
Of blessed consolations in distress;
Of moral strength, and intellectual Power;
Of joy in widest commonalty spread;
Of the individual mind that keeps her own
Inviolate retirement, subject there   20
To Conscience only, and the law supreme
Of that Intelligence which governs all—
I sing:—'fit audience let me find though few!'

So prayed, more gaining than he asked, the Bard—
In holiest mood. Urania, I shall need   25
Thy guidance, or a greater Muse, if such
Descend to earth or dwell in highest heaven!
For I must tread on shadowy ground, must sink

30

Deep—and, aloft ascending, breathe in worlds
To which the heaven of heavens is but a veil.   30
All strength—all terror, single or in bands,
That ever was put forth in personal form—
Jehovah—with his thunder, and the choir
Of shouting Angels, and the empyreal thrones—
I pass them unalarmed. Not Chaos, not   35
The darkest pit of lowest Erebus,
Nor aught of blinder vacancy, scooped out
By help of dreams—can breed such fear and awe
As fall upon us often when we look
Into our Minds, into the Mind of Man—   40
My haunt, and the main region of my song.
Beauty—a living Presence of the earth,
Surpassing the most fair ideal Forms
Which craft of delicate Spirits hath composed
From earth's materials—waits upon my steps;   45
Pitches her tents before me as I move,
An hourly neighbour. Paradise, and groves
Elysian, Fortunate Fields—like those of old
Sought in the Atlantic Main—why should they be
A history only of departed things,   50
Or a mere fiction of what never was?
For the discerning intellect of Man,
When wedded to this goodly universe
In love and holy passion, shall find these
A simple produce of the common day.   55
I, long before the blissful hour arrives,
Would chant, in lonely peace, the spousal verse
Of this great consummation:—and, by words
Which speak of nothing more than what we are,
Would I arouse the sensual from their sleep   60
Of Death, and win the vacant and the vain
To noble raptures; while my voice proclaims

How exquisitely the individual Mind
(And the progressive powers perhaps no less
Of the whole species) to the external World   65
Is fitted:—and how exquisitely, too—
Theme this but little heard of among men—
The external world is fitted to the Mind;
And the creation (by no lower name
Can it be called) which they with blended might   70
Accomplish:—this is our high argument.
—Such grateful haunts foregoing, if I oft
Must turn elsewhere—to travel near the tribes
And fellowships of men, and see ill sights
Of madding passions mutually inflamed;   75
Must hear Humanity in fields and groves
Pipe solitary anguish; or must hang
Brooding above the fierce confederate storm
Of sorrow, barricadoed evermore
Within the walls of cities—may these sounds   80
Have their authentic comment; that even these
Hearing, I be not downcast or forlorn!—
Descend, prophetic Spirit! that inspir'st
The human Soul of universal earth,
Dreaming on things to come; and dost possess   85
A metropolitan temple in the hearts
Of mighty Poets: upon me bestow
A gift of genuine insight; that my Song
With star-like virtue in its place may shine,
Shedding benignant influence, and secure,   90
Itself, from all malevolent effect
Of those mutations that extend their sway
Throughout the nether sphere!—And if with this
I mix more lowly matter; with the thing
Contemplated, describe the Mind and Man   95
Contemplating; and who, and what he was—

The transitory Being that beheld
This Vision; when and where, and how he lived;—
Be not this labour useless. If such theme
May sort with highest objects, then—dread Power!   100
Whose gracious favour is the primal source
Of all illumination,—may my Life
Express the image of a better time,
More wise desires, and simpler manners;—nurse
My Heart in genuine freedom:—all pure thoughts   105
Be with me;—so shall thy unfailing love
Guide, and support, and cheer me to the end.

From *Home at Grasmere*

(*Part* 1, *Book* I, of *The Recluse*)

I

Embrace me then, ye Hills, and close me in,
Now in the clear and open day I feel
Your guardianship; I take it to my heart;
'Tis like the solemn shelter of the night.
But I would call thee beautiful, for mild,   5
And soft, and gay, and beautiful thou art,
Dear Valley, having in thy face a smile
Though peaceful, full of gladness. Thou art pleased,
Pleased with thy crags, and woody steeps, thy Lake,
Its one green Island and its winding shores;   10
The multitude of little rocky hills,
Thy Church and Cottages of mountain stone
Clustered like stars some few, but single most,
And lurking dimly in their shy retreats,
Or glancing at each other chearful looks,   15
Like separated stars with clouds between.

What want we? have we not perpetual streams,
Warm woods, and sunny hills, and fresh green fields,
And mountains not less green, and flocks, and herds,
And thickets full of songsters, and the voice   20
Of lordly birds, an unexpected sound
Heard now and then from morn to latest eve,
Admonishing the man who walks below
Of solitude, and silence in the sky?
These have we, and a thousand nooks of earth   25
Have also these, but no where else is found,
No where (or is it fancy?) can be found
The one sensation that is here; 'tis here,
Here as it found its way into my heart
In childhood, here as it abides by day,   30
By night, here only; or in chosen minds
That take it with them hence, where'er they go.
'Tis, but I cannot name it, 'tis the sense
Of majesty, and beauty, and repose,
A blended holiness of earth and sky,   35
Something that makes this individual Spot,
This small Abiding-place of many Men,
A termination, and a last retreat,
A Centre, come from wheresoe'er you will,
A Whole without dependence or defect,   40
Made for itself; and happy in itself,
Perfect Contentment, Unity entire.

   Bleak season was it, turbulent and bleak,
When hitherward we journeyed, side by side,
Through bursts of sunshine and through flying showers, 45
Paced the long Vales, how long they were, and yet
How fast that length of way was left behind,
Wensley's rich Vale and Sedbergh's naked heights.
The frosty wind, as if to make amends

For its keen breath, was aiding to our steps,   50
And drove us onward like two ships at sea,
Or like two Birds, companions in mid air,
Parted and re-united by the blast.
Stern was the face of Nature; we rejoiced
In that stern countenance, for our Souls drew thence   55
A feeling of their strength. The naked Trees,
The icy brooks, as on we passed, appeared
To question us. 'Whence come ye? to what end?'
They seemed to say; 'What would ye,' said the shower,
'Wild Wanderers, whither through my dark domain?'   60
The sunbeam said, 'be happy.' When this Vale
We entered, bright and solemn was the sky
That faced us with a passionate welcoming,
And led us to our threshold. Daylight failed
Insensibly, and round us gently fell   65
Composing darkness, with a quiet load
Of full contentment, in a little Shed
Disturbed, uneasy in itself as seemed,
And wondering at its new inhabitants.
It loves us now, this Vale so beautiful   70
Begins to love us! By a sullen storm,
Two months unwearied of severest storm,
It put the temper of our minds to proof,
And found us faithful through the gloom, and heard
The Poet mutter his prelusive songs   75
With chearful heart, an unknown voice of joy,
Among the silence of the woods and hills;
Silent to any gladsomeness of sound
With all their Shepherds.

2

But not betrayed by tenderness of mind   80
That feared, or wholly overlook'd the truth,

Did we come hither, with romantic hope
To find, in midst of so much loveliness,
Love, perfect love; of so much majesty
A like majestic frame of mind in those   85
Who here abide, the persons like the place.
Not from such hope, or aught of such belief
Hath issued any portion of the joy
Which I have felt this day. An awful voice,
'Tis true, hath in my walks been often heard,   90
Sent from the mountains or the sheltered fields,
Shout after shout—reiterated whoop
In manner of a bird that takes delight
In answering to itself; or like a hound
Single at chase among the lonely woods,   95
His yell repeating; yet it was in truth
A human voice—a Spirit of coming night,
How solemn when the sky is dark, and earth
Not dark, nor yet enlightened, but by snow
Made visible, amid a noise of winds   100
And bleatings manifold of mountain sheep,
Which in that iteration recognize
Their summons, and are gathering round for food,
Devoured with keenness ere to grove or bank
Or rocky *bield* with patience they retire.   105

    That very voice, which in some timid mood
Of superstitious fancy, might have seemed
Awful as ever stray Demoniac uttered,
His steps to govern in the Wilderness;
Or as the Norman Curfew's regular beat,   110
To hearths when first they darkened at the knell:
That Shepherd's voice, it may have reached mine ear
Debased and under profanation, made
The ready Organ of articulate sounds

From ribaldry, impiety or wrath   115
Issuing when shame hath ceased to check the brawls
Of some abused Festivity—so be it.
I came not dreaming of unruffled life,
Untainted manners; born among the hills,
Bred also there, I wanted not a scale   120
To regulate my hopes. Pleased with the good,
I shrink not from the evil with disgust,
Or with immoderate pain. I look for Man,
The common Creature of the brotherhood,
Differing but little from the Man elsewhere,   125
For selfishness, and envy, and revenge,
Ill neighbourhood—pity that this should be—
Flattering and double-dealing, strife and wrong.

   Yet is it something gained, it is in truth
A mighty gain, that Labour here preserves   130
His rosy face, a Servant only here
Of the fire-side, or of the open field.
A Freeman, therefore, sound and unimpaired;
That extreme penury is here unknown,
And cold and hunger's abject wretchedness,   135
Mortal to body, and the heaven-born mind;
That they who want, are not too great a weight
For those who can relieve. Here may the heart
Breathe in the air of fellow-suffering
Dreadless, as in a kind of fresher breeze   140
Of her own native element, the hand
Be ready and unwearied without plea
From tasks too frequent, or beyond its power
For languor, or indifference, or despair.
And as these lofty barriers break the force   145
Of winds, this deep Vale,—as it doth in part
Conceal us from the Storm,—so here abides

A Power and a protection for the mind,
Dispensed indeed to other solitudes,
Favoured by noble privilege like this,
Where kindred independence of estate
Is prevalent, where he who tills the field,
He, happy Man! is Master of the field,
And treads the mountains which his Fathers trod.

Lines written in Early Spring

I heard a thousand blended notes,
While in a grove I sate reclined,
In that sweet mood when pleasant thoughts
Bring sad thoughts to the mind.

To her fair works did Nature link   5
The human soul that through me ran;
And much it grieved my heart to think
What man has made of man.

Through primrose tufts, in that green bower,
The periwinkle trailed its wreaths;   10
And 'tis my faith that every flower
Enjoys the air it breathes.

The birds around me hopped and played,
Their thoughts I cannot measure:—
But the least motion which they made,   15
It seemed a thrill of pleasure.

The budding twigs spread out their fan,
To catch the breezy air;
And I must think, do all I can,
That there was pleasure there.   20

If this belief from heaven be sent,
If such be Nature's holy plan,
Have I not reason to lament
What man has made of man?

Expostulation and Reply

'Why, William, on that old grey stone,
Thus for the length of half a day,
Why, William, sit you thus alone,
And dream your time away?

'Where are your books?—that light bequeathed   5
To Beings else forlorn and blind!
Up! up! and drink the spirit breathed
From dead men to their kind.

'You look round on your Mother Earth,
As if she for no purpose bore you;   10
As if you were her first-born birth,
And none had lived before you!'

One morning thus, by Esthwaite lake,
When life was sweet, I knew not why,
To me my good friend Matthew spake,   15
And thus I made reply:

'The eye—it cannot choose but see;
We cannot bid the ear be still;
Our bodies feel, where'er they be,
Against or with our will.   20

'Nor less I deem that there are Powers
Which of themselves our minds impress;
That we can feed this mind of ours
In a wise passiveness.

'Think you, 'mid all this mighty sum   25
Of things for ever speaking,
That nothing of itself will come,
But we must still be seeking?

'—Then ask not wherefore, here, alone,
Conversing as I may,   30
I sit upon this old grey stone,
And dream my time away.'

The Tables Turned

AN EVENING SCENE ON THE SAME SUBJECT

Up! up! my Friend, and quit your books;
Or surely you'll grow double:
Up! up! my Friend, and clear your looks;
Why all this toil and trouble?

The sun, above the mountain's head,   5
A freshening lustre mellow
Through all the long green fields has spread,
His first sweet evening yellow.

Books! 'tis a dull and endless strife:
Come, hear the woodland linnet,   10
How sweet his music! on my life,
There's more of wisdom in it.

And hark! how blithe the throstle sings!
He, too, is no mean preacher:

Come forth into the light of things,   15
Let Nature be your Teacher.

She has a world of ready wealth,
Our minds and hearts to bless—
Spontaneous wisdom breathed by health,
Truth breathed by cheerfulness.   20

One impulse from a vernal wood
May teach you more of man,
Of moral evil and of good,
Than all the sages can.

Sweet is the lore which Nature brings;   25
Our meddling intellect
Mis-shapes the beauteous forms of things:—
We murder to dissect.

Enough of Science and of Art;
Close up those barren leaves;   30
Come forth, and bring with you a heart
That watches and receives.

Animal Tranquillity and Decay

The little hedgerow birds,
That peck along the road, regard him not.
He travels on, and in his face, his step,
His gait, is one expression: every limb,
His look and bending figure, all bespeak   5
A man who does not move with pain, but moves
With thought.—He is insensibly subdued

To settled quiet: he is one by whom
All effort seems forgotten; one to whom
Long patience hath such mild composure given,   10
That patience now doth seem a thing of which
He hath no need. He is by nature led
To peace so perfect that the young behold
With envy, what the Old Man hardly feels.
—I asked him whether he was bound, and what   15
The object of his journey; he replied
That he was going many miles to take
A last leave of his son, a mariner,
Who from a sea-fight had been brought to Falmouth,
And there was dying in an hospital.

The Thorn

I

'There is a Thorn—it looks so old,
In truth, you'd find it hard to say
How it could ever have been young,
It looks so old and grey.
Not higher than a two years' child   5
It stands erect, this aged Thorn;
No leaves it has, no prickly points;
It is a mass of knotted joints,
A wretched thing forlorn.
It stands erect, and like a stone   10
With lichens is it overgrown.

II

'Like rock or stone, it is o'ergrown,
With lichens to the very top,

And hung with heavy tufts of moss,
A melancholy crop: 15
Up from the earth these mosses creep,
And this poor Thorn they clasp it round
So close, you'd say that they are bent
With plain and manifest intent
To drag it to the ground;   20
And all have joined in one endeavour
To bury this poor Thorn for ever.

III

'High on a mountain's highest ridge,
Where oft the stormy winter gale
Cuts like a scythe, while through the clouds   25
It sweeps from vale to vale;
Not five yards from the mountain path,
This Thorn you on your left espy;
And to the left, three yards beyond,
You see a little muddy pond   30
Of water—never dry,
I've measured it from side to side;
'Tis three feet long, and two feet wide.

IV

'And, close beside this aged Thorn,
There is a fresh and lovely sight,   35
A beauteous heap, a hill of moss,
Just half a foot in height.
All lovely colours there you see,
All colours that were ever seen;
And mossy network too is there,   40
As if by hand of lady fair
The work had woven been;

And cups, the darlings of the eye,
So deep is their vermilion dye.

V

'Ah me! what lovely tints are there   45
Of olive green and scarlet bright,
In spikes, in branches, and in stars,
Green, red, and pearly white!
This heap of earth o'ergrown with moss,
Which close beside the Thorn you see,   50
So fresh in all its beauteous dyes,
Is like an infant's grave in size,
As like as like can be:
But never, never any where,
An infant's grave was half so fair.   55

VI

'Now would you see this aged Thorn,
This pond, and beauteous hill of moss,
You must take care and choose your time
The mountain when to cross.
For oft there sits between the heap,   60
That's like an infant's grave in size,
And that same pond of which I spoke,
A Woman in a scarlet cloak,
And to herself she cries,
"Oh misery! Oh misery!   65
Oh woe is me! oh misery!"

VII

'At all times of the day and night
This wretched Woman thither goes;

And she is known to every star,
And every wind that blows;   70
And there, beside the Thorn, she sits
When the blue daylight's in the skies,
And when the whirlwind's on the hill,
Or frosty air is keen and still,
And to herself she cries,   75
"Oh misery! oh misery!
Oh woe is me! oh misery!" '

VIII

'Now wherefore, thus, by day and night,
In rain, in tempest, and in snow,
Thus to the dreary mountain-top   80
Does this poor Woman go?
And why sits she beside the Thorn
When the blue daylight's in the sky
Or when the whirlwind's on the hill,
Or frosty air is keen and still,   85
And wherefore does she cry?—
O wherefore? wherefore? tell me why
Does she repeat that doleful cry?'

IX

'I cannot tell; I wish I knew;
For the true reason no one knows: 90
But would you gladly view the spot,
The spot to which she goes;
The heap that's like an infant's grave,
The pond—and Thorn, so old and grey;
Pass by her door—'tis seldom shut—   95
And if you see her in her hut—
Then to the spot away!

I never heard of such as dare
Approach the spot when she is there.'

X

'But wherefore to the mountain-top   100
Can this unhappy woman go,
Whatever star is in the skies,
Whatever wind may blow?'
'Tis now some two and twenty years
Since she (her name is Martha Ray)   105
Gave with a maiden's true good-will
Her company to Stephen Hill;
And she was blithe and gay,
And she was happy, happy still
Whene'er she thought of Stephen Hill.   110

XI

'And they had fixed the wedding day,
The morning that must wed them both;
But Stephen to another maid
Had sworn another oath;
And, with this other Maid, to church,   115
Unthinking Stephen went—
Poor Martha! on that woeful day
A pang of pitiless dismay
Into her soul was sent;
A fire was kindled in her breast,   120
Which might not burn itself to rest.

XII

'They say, full six months after this,
While yet the summer leaves were green
She to the mountain-top would go,

And there was often seen. 125
'Tis said, a child was in her womb,
As now to any eye was plain;
She was with child, and she was mad;
Yet often was she sober sad
From her exceeding pain. 130
Oh me, ten thousand times I'd rather
That he had died, that cruel father!

XIII

'Sad case for such a brain to hold
Communion with a stirring child!
Sad case, as you may think, for one 135
Who had a brain so wild!
Last Christmas when we talked of this,
Old Father Simpson did maintain
That in her womb the infant wrought
About its mother's heart, and brought 140
Her senses back again:
And, when at last her time drew near,
Her looks were calm, her senses clear.

XIV

'No more I know, I wish I did,
And I would tell it all to you; 145
For what became of this poor child
There's none that ever knew:
And if a child was born or no,
There's no one that could ever tell;
And if 'twas born alive or dead, 150
There's no one knows, as I have said;
But some remember well,
That Martha Ray about this time
Would up the mountain often climb.

XV

'And all that winter, when at night   155
The wind blew from the mountain-peak,
'Twas worth your while, though in the dark,
The church-yard path to seek:
For many a time and oft were heard
Cries coming from the mountain head: 160
Some plainly living voices were:
And others, I've heard many swear,
Were voices of the dead:
I cannot think, whate'er they say,
They had to do with Martha Ray.   165

XVI

'But that she goes to this old Thorn,
The Thorn which I described to you,
And there sits in a scarlet cloak,
I will be sworn is true.
For one day with my telescope,   170
To view the ocean wide and bright,
When to this country first I came,
Ere I had heard of Martha's name,
I climbed the mountain's height:—
A storm came on, and I could see   175
No object higher than my knee.

XVII

' 'Twas mist and rain, and storm and rain;
No screen, no fence could I discover;
And then the wind! in faith, it was
A wind full ten times over.   180
I looked around, I thought I saw

A jutting crag,—and off I ran,
Head-foremost, through the driving rain,
The shelter of the crag to gain;
And, as I am a man,   185
Instead of jutting crag, I found
A Woman seated on the ground.

XVII

'I did not speak—I saw her face;
Her face!—it was enough for me;
I turned about and heard her cry,   190
"Oh misery! oh misery!"
And there she sits, until the moon
Through half the clear blue sky will go;
And when the little breezes make
The waters of the pond to shake,   195
As all the country know,
She shudders, and you hear her cry,
"Oh misery! oh misery!"

XIX

'But what's the Thorn? and what's the pond?
And what's the hill of moss to her?   200
And what's the creeping breeze that comes
The little pond to stir?'
'I cannot tell; but some will say
She hanged her baby on the tree;
Some say she drowned it in the pond,   205
Which is a little step beyond:
But all and each agree,
The little Babe was buried there,
Beneath that hill of moss so fair.

XX

'I've heard, the moss is spotted red   210
With drops of that poor infant's blood;
But kill a new-born infant thus,
I do not think she could!
Some say, if to the pond you go,
And fix on it a steady view,   215
The shadow of a babe you trace,
A baby and a baby's face,
And that it looks at you;
Whene'er you look on it, 'tis plain
The baby looks at you again.   220

XXI

'And some had sworn an oath that she
Should be to public justice brought;
And for the little infant's bones
With spades they would have sought.
But then the beauteous hill of moss   225
Before their eyes began to stir!
And, for full fifty yards around,
The grass—it shook upon the ground!
Yet all do still aver
The little Babe lies buried there,   230
Beneath that hill of moss so fair

XXII

'I cannot tell how this may be,
But plain it is the Thorn is bound
With heavy tufts of moss that strive
To drag it to the ground;   235
And this I know, full many a time,

When she was on the mountain high,
By day, and in the silent night,
When all the stars shone clear and bright,
That I have heard her cry,   240
"Oh misery! oh misery!
Oh woe is me! oh misery!"

Tintern Abbey

*Lines composed a few miles above Tintern Abbey, on revisiting
the banks of the Wye during a Tour.   July 13, 1798.*

Five years have past; five summers, with the length
Of five long winters! and again I hear
These waters, rolling from their mountain-springs
With a soft inland murmur.—Once again
Do I behold these steep and lofty cliffs,   5
That on a wild secluded scene impress
Thoughts of more deep seclusion; and connect
The landscape with the quiet of the sky.
The day is come when I again repose
Here, under this dark sycamore, and view   10
These plots of cottage-ground, these orchard-tufts,
Which at this season, with their unripe fruits,
Are clad in one green hue, and lose themselves
'Mid groves and copses. Once again I see
These hedge-rows, hardly hedge-rows, little lines   15
Of sportive wood run wild: these pastoral farms,
Green to the very door: and wreaths of smoke
Sent up, in silence, from among the trees!
With some uncertain notice, as might seem

Of vagrant dwellers in the houseless woods,   20
Or of some Hermit's cave, where by his fire
The Hermit sits alone.

                              These beauteous forms
Through a long absence, have not been to me
As is a landscape to a blind man's eye: 25
But oft, in lonely rooms, and 'mid the din
Of towns and cities, I have owed to them,
In hours of weariness, sensations sweet,
Felt in the blood, and felt along the heart;
And passing even into my purer mind,   30
With tranquil restoration:—feelings too
Of unremembered pleasure: such, perhaps,
As have no slight or trivial influence
On that best portion of a good man's life,
His little, nameless, unremembered, acts   35
Of kindness and of love. Nor less, I trust,
To them I may have owed another gift,
Of aspect more sublime; that blessed mood,
In which the burthen of the mystery,
In which the heavy and the weary weight   40
Of all this unintelligible world,
Is lightened:—that serene and blessed mood,
In which the affections gently lead us on,—
Until, the breath of this corporeal frame
And even the motion of our human blood   45
Almost suspended, we are laid asleep
In body, and become a living soul:
While with an eye made quiet by the power
Of harmony, and the deep power of joy,
We see into the life of things.   50
                              If this
Be but a vain belief, yet, oh! how oft—

In darkness and amid the many shapes
Of joyless daylight; when the fretful stir
Unprofitable, and the fever of the world,   55
Have hung upon the beatings of my heart—
How oft, in spirit, have I turned to thee,
O sylvan Wye! thou wanderer thro' the woods,
How often has my spirit turned to thee!

   And now, with gleams of half-extinguished thought,   60
With many recognitions dim and faint,
And somewhat of a sad perplexity,
The picture of the mind revives again:
While here I stand, not only with the sense
Of present pleasure, but with pleasing thoughts   65
That in this moment there is life and food
For future years. And so I dare to hope,
Though changed, no doubt, from what I was when first
I came among these hills; when like a roe
I bounded o'er the mountains, by the sides   70
Of the deep rivers, and the lonely streams,
Wherever nature led: more like a man
Flying from something that he dreads than one
Who sought the thing he loved. For nature then
(The coarser pleasures of my boyish days,   75
And their glad animal movements all gone by)
To me was all in all.—I cannot paint
What then I was. The sounding cataract
Haunted me like a passion: the tall rock,
The mountain, and the deep and gloomy wood,   80
Their colours and their forms, were then to me
An appetite; a feeling and a love,
That had no need of a remoter charm,
By thought supplied, nor any interest
Unborrowed from the eye.—That time is past,   85

And all its aching joys are now no more,
And all its dizzy raptures. Not for this
Faint I, nor mourn nor murmur; other gifts
Have followed; for such loss, I would believe,
Abundant recompense. For I have learned   90
To look on nature, not as in the hour
Of thoughtless youth; but hearing oftentimes
The still, sad music of humanity,
Nor harsh nor grating, though of ample power
To chasten and subdue. And I have felt   95
A presence that disturbs me with the joy
Of elevated thoughts; a sense sublime
Of something far more deeply interfused,
Whose dwelling is the light of setting suns,
And the round ocean and the living air,   100
And the blue sky, and in the mind of man:
A motion and a spirit, that impels
All thinking things, all objects of all thought,
And rolls through all things. Therefore am I still
A lover of the meadows and the woods,   105
And mountains; and of all that we behold
From this green earth; of all the mighty world
Of eye, and ear,—both what they half create,
And what perceive; well pleased to recognize
In nature and the language of the sense   110
The anchor of my purest thoughts, the nurse,
The guide, the guardian of my heart, and soul
Of all my moral being.
                              Nor perchance,
If I were not thus taught, should I the more   115
Suffer my genial spirits to decay:
For thou art with me here upon the banks
Of this fair river; thou my dearest Friend,
My dear, dear Friend; and in thy voice I catch

The language of my former heart, and read   120
My former pleasures in the shooting lights
Of thy wild eyes. Oh! yet a little while
May I behold in thee what I was once,
My dear, dear Sister! and this prayer I make,
Knowing that Nature never did betray   125
The heart that loved her; 'tis her privilege,
Through all the years of this our life, to lead
From joy to joy: for she can so inform
The mind that is within us, so impress
With quietness and beauty, and so feed   130
With lofty thoughts, that neither evil tongues,
Rash judgments, nor the sneers of selfish men,
Nor greetings where no kindness is, nor all
The dreary intercourse of daily life,
Shall e'er prevail against us, or disturb   135
Our cheerful faith, that all which we behold
Is full of blessings. Therefore let the moon
Shine on thee in thy solitary walk;
And let the misty mountain-winds be free
To blow against thee: and, in after years,   140
When these wild ecstasies shall be matured
Into a sober pleasure; when thy mind
Shall be a mansion for all lovely forms,
Thy memory be as a dwelling-place
For all sweet sounds and harmonies; oh! then,   145
If solitude, or fear, or pain, or grief,
Should be thy portion, with what healing thoughts
Of tender joy wilt thou remember me,
And these my exhortations! Nor, perchance—
If I should be where I no more can hear   150
Thy voice, nor catch from thy wild eyes these gleams
Of past existence—wilt thou then forget
That on the banks of this delightful stream

We stood together; and that I, so long
A worshipper of Nature, hither came   155
Unwearied in that service: rather say
With warmer love—oh! with far deeper zeal
Of holier love. Nor wilt thou then forget
That after many wanderings, many years
Of absence, these steep woods and lofty cliffs,   160
And this green pastoral landscape, were to me
More dear, both for themselves and for thy sake!

The Reverie of Poor Susan

At the corner of Wood Street, when daylight appears,
Hangs a Thrush that sings loud, it has sung for three years:
Poor Susan has passed by the spot, and has heard
In the silence of morning the song of the Bird.

'Tis a note of enchantment; what ails her? She sees   5
A mountain ascending, a vision of trees;
Bright volumes of vapour through Lothbury glide,
And a river flows on through the vale of Cheapside.

Green pastures she views in the midst of the dale,
Down which she so often has tripped with her pail;   10
And a single small cottage, a nest like a dove's,
The one only dwelling on earth that she loves.

She looks, and her heart is in heaven: but they fade,
The mist and the river, the hill and the shade:
The stream will not flow, and the hill will not rise,   15
And the colours have all passed away from her eyes!

Lucy Poems

I

Strange fits of passion have I known:
And I will dare to tell,
But in the Lover's ear alone,
What once to me befell.

When she I loved looked every day   5
Fresh as a rose in June,
I to her cottage bent my way,
Beneath an evening-moon.

Upon the moon I fixed my eye,
All over the wide lea;   10
With quickening pace my horse drew nigh
Those paths so dear to me.

And now we reached the orchard-plot;
And, as we climbed the hill,
The sinking moon to Lucy's cot   15
Came near, and nearer still.

In one of those sweet dreams I slept,
Kind Nature's gentlest boon!
And all the while my eyes I kept
On the descending moon.   20

My horse moved on; hoof after hoof
He raised, and never stopped:

When down behind the cottage roof,
At once, the bright moon dropped.

What fond and wayward thoughts will slide   25
Into a Lover's head!
'O mercy!' to myself I cried,
'If Lucy should be dead!'

II

I travelled among unknown men,
    In lands beyond the sea;
Nor, England! did I know till then
    What love I bore to thee.

'Tis past, that melancholy dream!   5
    Nor will I quit thy shore
A second time; for still I seem
    To love thee more and more.

Among thy mountains did I feel
    The joy of my desire;   10
And she I cherished turned her wheel
    Beside an English fire.

Thy mornings showed, thy nights concealed,
    The bowers where Lucy played;
And thine too is the last green field   15
    That Lucy's eyes surveyed.

III

Three years she grew in sun and shower,
Then Nature said, 'A lovelier flower
On earth was never sown;

This Child I to myself will take;
She shall be mine, and I will make   5
A Lady of my own.

'Myself will to my darling be
Both law and impulse: and with me
The Girl, in rock and plain,
In earth and heaven, in glade and bower,   10
Shall feel an overseeing power
To kindle or restrain.

'She shall be sportive as the fawn
That wild with glee across the lawn
Or up the mountain springs;   15
And hers shall be the breathing balm,
And hers the silence and the calm
Of mute insensate things.

'The floating clouds their state shall lend
To her; for her the willow bend;   20
Nor shall she fail to see
Even in the motions of the Storm
Grace that shall mould the Maiden's form
By silent sympathy.

'The stars of midnight shall be dear   25
To her; and she shall lean her ear
In many a secret place
Where rivulets dance their wayward round,
And beauty born of murmuring sound
Shall pass into her face.   30

'And vital feelings of delight
Shall rear her form to stately height,

Her virgin bosom swell;
Such thoughts to Lucy I will give
While she and I together live   35
Here in this happy dell.'

Thus Nature spake—The work was done—
How soon my Lucy's race was run!
She died, and left to me
This heath, this calm, and quiet scene;   40
The memory of what has been,
And never more will be.

IV

She dwelt among the untrodden ways
    Beside the springs of Dove,
A Maid whom there were none to praise
    And very few to love:

A violet by a mossy stone   5
    Half hidden from the eye!
—Fair as a star, when only one
    Is shining in the sky.

She lived unknown, and few could know
    When Lucy ceased to be;   10
But she is in her grave, and, oh,
    The difference to me!

V

A slumber did my spirit seal;
    I had no human fears:
She seemed a thing that could not feel
    The touch of earthly years.

No motion has she now, no force;   5
   She neither hears nor sees;
Rolled round in earth's diurnal course,
   With rocks, and stones, and trees.

Lucy Gray

or, Solitude

Oft I had heard of Lucy Gray:
And, when I crossed the wild,
I chanced to see at break of day
The solitary child.

No mate, no comrade Lucy knew;   5
She dwelt on a wide moor,
—The sweetest thing that ever grew
Beside a human door!

You yet may spy the fawn at play,
The hare upon the green;   10
But the sweet face of Lucy Gray
Will never more be seen.

'To-night will be a stormy night—
You to the town must go;
And take a lantern, Child, to light   15
Your mother through the snow.'

'That, Father! will I gladly do:
'Tis scarcely afternoon—
The minster-clock has just struck two,
And yonder is the moon!'   20

At this the Father raised his hook,
And snapped a faggot-band;
He plied his work;—and Lucy took
The lantern in her hand.

Not blither is the mountain roe: 25
With many a wanton stroke
Her feet disperse the powdery snow,
That rises up like smoke.

The storm came on before its time:
She wandered up and down;   30
And many a hill did Lucy climb:
But never reached the town.

The wretched parents all that night
Went shouting far and wide;
But there was neither sound nor sight   35
To serve them for a guide.

At day-break on a hill they stood
That overlooked the moor;
And thence they saw the bridge of wood,
A furlong from their door.   40

They wept—and, turning homeward, cried,
'In heaven we all shall meet';
—When in the snow the mother spied
The print of Lucy's feet.

Then downwards from the steep hill's edge   45
They tracked the footmarks small;
And through the broken hawthorn hedge,
And by the long stone-wall;

And then an open field they crossed:
The marks were still the same;   50
They tracked them on, nor ever lost;
And to the bridge they came.

They followed from the snowy bank
Those footmarks, one by one,
Into the middle of the plank;   55
And further there were none!

—Yet some maintain that to this day
She is a living child;
That you may see sweet Lucy Gray
Upon the lonesome wild.   60

O'er rough and smooth she trips along,
And never looks behind;
And sings a solitary song
That whistles in the wind.

Nutting

———————It seems a day
(I speak of one from many singled out)
One of those heavenly days that cannot die;
When, in the eagerness of boyish hope,
I left our cottage-threshold, sallying forth   5
With a huge wallet o'er my shoulders slung,
A nutting-crook in hand; and turned my steps
Tow'rd some far-distant wood, a Figure quaint,
Tricked out in proud disguise of cast-off weeds

Which for that service had been husbanded,   10
By exhortation of my frugal Dame—
Motley accoutrement, of power to smile
At thorns, and brakes, and brambles,—and in truth
More ragged than need was! O'er pathless rocks,
Through beds of matted fern, and tangled thickets,   15
Forcing my way, I came to one dear nook
Unvisited, where not a broken bough
Drooped with its withered leaves, ungracious sign
Of devastation; but the hazels rose
Tall and erect, with tempting clusters hung,   20
A virgin scene!—A little while I stood,
Breathing with such suppression of the heart
As joy delights in; and with wise restraint
Voluptuous, fearless of a rival, eyed
The banquet;—or beneath the trees I sate   25
Among the flowers, and with the flowers I played;
A temper known to those who, after long
And weary expectation, have been blest
With sudden happiness beyond all hope.
Perhaps it was a bower beneath whose leaves   30
The violets of five seasons re-appear
And fade, unseen by any human eye;
Where fairy water-breaks do murmur on
For ever; and I saw the sparkling foam,
And with my cheek on one of those green stones   35
That, fleeced with moss, under the shady trees,
Lay round me, scattered like a flock of sheep—
I heard the murmur and the murmuring sound,
In that sweet mood when pleasure loves to pay
Tribute to ease; and, of its joy secure,   40
The heart luxuriates with indifferent things,
Wasting its kindliness on stocks and stones,
And on the vacant air. Then up I rose,

And dragged to earth both branch and bough, with crash
And merciless ravage: and the shady nook   45
Of hazels, and the green and mossy bower,
Deformed and sullied, patiently gave up
Their quiet being: and unless I now
Confound my present feelings with the past,
Ere from the mutilated bower I turned   50
Exulting, rich beyond the wealth of kings,
I felt a sense of pain when I beheld
The silent trees, and saw the intruding sky.—
Then, dearest Maiden, move along these shades
In gentleness of heart; with gentle hand   55
Touch—for there is a spirit in the woods.

'A whirl-blast from behind the hill'

A whirl-blast from behind the hill
Rushed o'er the wood with startling sound;
Then—all at once the air was still,
And showers of hailstones pattered round.
Where leafless oaks towered high above,   5
I sat within an undergrove
Of tallest hollies, tall and green;
A fairer bower was never seen.
From year to year the spacious floor
With withered leaves is covered o'er,   10
And all the year the bower is green.
   But see! where'er the hailstones drop
The withered leaves all skip and hop;
There's not a breeze—no breath of air—
Yet here, and there, and every where   15

Along the floor, beneath the shade
By those embowering hollies made,
The leaves in myriads jump and spring,
As if with pipes and music rare
Some Robin Good-fellow were there,   20
And all those leaves, in festive glee
Were dancing to the minstrelsy.

Michael

If from the public way you turn your steps
Up the tumultuous brook of Greenhead Ghyll,
You will suppose that with an upright path
Your feet must struggle; in such bold ascent
The pastoral mountains front you, face to face.   5
But, courage! for around that boisterous brook
The mountains have all opened out themselves,
And made a hidden valley of their own.
No habitation can be seen; but they
Who journey thither find themselves alone   10
With a few sheep, with rocks and stones, and kites
That over head are sailing in the sky.
It is in truth an utter solitude;
Nor should I have made mention of this Dell
But for one object which you might pass by,   15
Might see and notice not. Beside the brook
Appears a straggling heap of unhewn stones!
And to that simple object appertains
A story—unenriched with strange events,
Yet not unfit, I deem, for the fireside,   20
Or for the summer shade. It was the first
Of those domestic tales that spake to me
Of shepherds, dwellers in the valleys, men
Whom I already loved; not verily
For their own sakes, but for the fields and hills   25
Where was their occupation and abode.
And hence this Tale, while I was yet a Boy
Careless of books, yet having felt the power
Of Nature, by the gentle agency

Of natural objects, led me on to feel   30
For passions that were not my own, and think
(At random and imperfectly indeed)
On man, the heart of man, and human life.
Therefore, although it be a history
Homely and rude, I will relate the same   35
For the delight of a few natural hearts;
And, with yet fonder feeling, for the sake
Of youthful Poets, who among these hills
Will be my second self when I am gone.
    Upon the forest-side in Grasmere Vale   40
There dwelt a Shepherd, Michael was his name;
An old man, stout of heart, and strong of limb.
His bodily frame had been from youth to age
Of an unusual strength: his mind was keen,
Intense, and frugal, apt for all affairs,   45
And in his shepherd's calling he was prompt
And watchful more than ordinary men.
Hence had he learned the meaning of all winds,
Of blasts of every tone; and, oftentimes,
When others heeded not, He heard the South   50
Make subterraneous music, like the noise
Of bagpipers on distant Highland hills.
The Shepherd, at such warning, of his flock
Bethought him, and he to himself would say,
'The winds are now devising work for me!'   55
And, truly, at all times, the storm, that drives
The traveller to a shelter, summoned him
Up to the mountains: he had been alone
Amid the heart of many thousand mists,
That came to him, and left him, on the heights.   60
So lived he till his eightieth year was past.
And grossly that man errs, who should suppose
That the green valleys, and the streams and rocks,

Were things indifferent to the Shepherd's thoughts.
Fields, where with cheerful spirits he had breathed 65
The common air; hills, which with vigorous step
He had so often climbed; which had impressed
So many incidents upon his mind
Of hardship, skill or courage, joy or fear;
Which, like a book, preserved the memory 70
Of the dumb animals, whom he had saved,
Had fed or sheltered, linking to such acts
The certainty of honourable gain;
Those fields, those hills—what could they less? had laid
Strong hold on his affections, were to him 75
A pleasurable feeling of blind love,
The pleasure which there is in life itself.
    His days had not been passed in singleness.
His Helpmate was a comely matron, old—
Though younger than himself full twenty years. 80
She was a woman of a stirring life,
Whose heart was in her house: two wheels she had
Of antique form; this large, for spinning wool;
That small, for flax; and if one wheel had rest
It was because the other was at work. 85
The Pair had but one inmate in their house,
An only Child, who had been born to them
When Michael, telling o'er his years, began
To deem that he was old,—in shepherd's phrase,
With one foot in the grave. This only Son, 90
With two brave sheep-dogs tried in many a storm,
The one of an inestimable worth,
Made all their household. I may truly say,
That they were as a proverb in the vale
For endless industry. When day was gone, 95
And from their occupations out of doors
The Son and Father were come home, even then,

Their labour did not cease; unless when all
Turned to the cleanly supper-board, and there,
Each with a mess of pottage and skimmed milk,   100
Sat round the basket piled with oaten cakes,
And their plain home-made cheese. Yet when the meal
Was ended, Luke (for so the Son was named)
And his old Father both betook themselves
To such convenient work as might employ   105
Their hands by the fireside; perhaps to card
Wool for the Housewife's spindle, or repair
Some injury done to sickle, flail, or scythe,
Or other implement of house or field.
    Down from the ceiling, by the chimney's edge,   110
That in our ancient uncouth country style
With huge and black projection overbrowed
Large space beneath, as duly as the light
Of day grew dim the Housewife hung a lamp;
An aged utensil, which had performed   115
Service beyond all others of its kind.
Early at evening did it burn—and late,
Surviving comrade of uncounted hours,
Which, going by from year to year, had found,
And left, the couple neither gay perhaps   120
Nor cheerful, yet with objects and with hopes,
Living a life of eager industry.
And now, when Luke had reached his eighteenth year,
There by the light of this old lamp they sate,
Father and Son, while far into the night   125
The Housewife plied her own peculiar work,
Making the cottage through the silent hours
Murmur as with the sound of summer flies.
This light was famous in its neighbourhood,
And was a public symbol of the life   130
That thrifty Pair had lived. For, as it chanced,

Their cottage on a plot of rising ground
Stood single, with large prospect, north and south,
High into Easedale, up to Dunmail-Raise,
And westward to the village near the lake;   135
And from this constant light, so regular
And so far seen, the House itself, by all
Who dwelt within the limits of the vale,
Both old and young, was named THE EVENING STAR.

    Thus living on through such a length of years,   140
The Shepherd, if he loved himself, must needs
Have loved his Helpmate; but to Michael's heart
This son of his old age was yet more dear—
Less from instinctive tenderness, the same
Fond spirit that blindly works in the blood of all—   145
Than that a child, more than all other gifts
That earth can offer to declining man,
Brings hope with it, and forward-looking thoughts,
And stirrings of inquietude, when they
By tendency of nature needs must fail.   150
Exceeding was the love he bare to him,
His heart and his heart's joy! For often-times
Old Michael, while he was a babe in arms,
Had done him female service, not alone
For pastime and delight, as is the use   155
Of fathers, but with patient mind enforced
To acts of tenderness; and he had rocked
His cradle, as with a woman's gentle hand.

    And, in a later time, ere yet the Boy
Had put on boy's attire, did Michael love,   160
Albeit of a stern unbending mind,
To have the Young-one in his sight, when he
Wrought in the field, or on his shepherd's stool
Sate with a fettered sheep before him stretched
Under the large old oak, that near his door   165

Stood single, and, from matchless depth of shade,
Chosen for the Shearer's covert from the sun,
Thence in our rustic dialect was called
The CLIPPING TREE,[1] a name which yet it bears.
There, while they two were sitting in the shade,   170
With others round them, earnest all and blithe,
Would Michael exercise his heart with looks
Of fond correction and reproof bestowed
Upon the Child, if he disturbed the sheep
By catching at their legs, or with his shouts   175
Scared them, while they lay still beneath the shears.
    And when by Heaven's good grace the boy grew up
A healthy Lad, and carried in his cheek
Two steady roses that were five years old;
Then Michael from a winter coppice cut   180
With his own hand a sapling, which he hooped
With iron, making it throughout in all
Due requisites a perfect shepherd's staff,
And gave it to the Boy; wherewith equipt
He as a watchman oftentimes was placed   185
At gate or gap, to stem or turn the flock;
And, to his office prematurely called,
There stood the urchin, as you will divine,
Something between a hindrance and a help;
And for this cause not always, I believe,   190
Receiving from his Father hire of praise;
Though nought was left undone which staff, or voice,
Or looks, or threatening gestures, could perform.
    But soon as Luke, full ten years old, could stand
Against the mountain blasts; and to the heights,   195
Not fearing toil, nor length of weary ways,
He with his Father daily went, and they
Were as companions, why should I relate

[1] Clipping is the word used in the North of England for shearing

That objects which the Shepherd loved before
Were dearer now? that from the Boy there came   200
Feelings and emanations—things which were
Light to the sun and music to the wind;
And that the old Man's heart seemed born again?
    Thus in his Father's sight the Boy grew up:
And now, when he had reached his eighteenth year   205
He was his comfort and his daily hope.
    While in this sort the simple household lived
From day to day, to Michael's ear there came
Distressful tidings. Long before the time
Of which I speak, the Shepherd had been bound   210
In surety for his brother's son, a man
Of an industrious life, and ample means;
But unforeseen misfortunes suddenly
Had prest upon him; and old Michael now
Was summoned to discharge the forfeiture,   215
A grievous penalty, but little less
Than half his substance. This unlooked-for claim,
At the first hearing, for a moment took
More hope out of his life than he supposed
That any old man ever could have lost.   220
As soon as he had armed himself with strength
To look his trouble in the face, it seemed
The Shepherd's sole resource to sell at once
A portion of his patrimonial fields.
Such was his first resolve; he thought again,   225
And his heart failed him. 'Isabel,' said he,
Two evenings after he had heard the news,
'I have been toiling more than seventy years,
And in the open sunshine of God's love
Have we all lived: yet if these fields of ours   230
Should pass into a stranger's hand, I think
That I could not lie quiet in my grave.

Our lot is a hard lot; the sun himself
Has scarcely been more diligent than I;
And I have lived to be a fool at last   235
To my own family. An evil man
That was, and made an evil choice, if he
Were false to us; and if he were not false,
There are ten thousand to whom loss like this
Had been no sorrow. I forgive him;—but   240
'Twere better to be dumb than to talk thus.
    'When I began, my purpose was to speak
Of remedies and of a cheerful hope.
Our Luke shall leave us, Isabel; the land
Shall not go from us, and it shall be free;   245
He shall possess it, free as is the wind
That passes over it. We have, thou know'st,
Another kinsman—he will be our friend
In this distress. He is a prosperous man,
Thriving in trade—and Luke to him shall go,   250
And with his kinsman's help and his own thrift
He quickly will repair this loss, and then
He may return to us. If here he stay,
What can be done? Where every one is poor,   255
What can be gained?'
                          At this the old Man paused,
And Isabel sat silent, for her mind
Was busy, looking back into past times.
There's Richard Bateman, thought she to herself,
He was a parish-boy—at the church-door   260
They made a gathering for him, shillings, pence
And halfpennies, wherewith the neighbours bought
A basket, which they filled with pedlar's wares;
And, with this basket on his arm, the lad
Went up to London, found a master there,   265
Who, out of many, chose the trusty boy

75

To go and overlook his merchandise
Beyond the seas; where he grew wondrous rich,
And left estates and monies to the poor.
And, at his birth-place, built a chapel, floored   270
With marble which he sent from foreign lands.
These thoughts, and many others of like sort,
Passed quickly through the mind of Isabel,
And her face brightened. The old Man was glad,
And thus resumed:—'Well, Isabel! this scheme   275
These two days, has been meat and drink to me.
Far more than we have lost is left us yet.
—We have enough—I wish indeed that I
Were younger;—but this hope is a good hope.
—Make ready Luke's best garments, of the best   280
Buy for him more, and let us send him forth
To-morrow, or the next day, or to-night:
—If he *could* go, the Boy should go to-night'.
    Here Michael ceased, and to the fields went forth
With a light heart. The Housewife for five days   285
Was restless morn and night, and all day long
Wrought on with her best fingers to prepare
Things needful for the journey of her son.
But Isabel was glad when Sunday came
To stop her in her work: for, when she lay   290
By Michael's side, she through the last two nights
Heard him, how he was troubled in his sleep:
And when they rose at morning she could see
That all his hopes were gone. That day at noon
She said to Luke, while they two by themselves   295
Were sitting at the door, 'Thou must not go:
We have no other Child but thee to lose,
None to remember—do not go away,
For if thou leave thy Father he will die'.
The Youth made answer with a jocund voice;   300

76

And Isabel, when she had told her fears,
Recovered heart. That evening her best fare
Did she bring forth, and all together sat
Like happy people round a Christmas fire.

    With daylight Isabel resumed her work; 305
And all the ensuing week the house appeared
As cheerful as a grove in Spring: at length
The expected letter from their kinsman came,
With kind assurances that he would do
His utmost for the welfare of the Boy; 310
To which, requests were added, that forthwith
He might be sent to him. Ten times or more
The letter was read over; Isabel
Went forth to show it to the neighbours round;
Nor was there at that time on English land 315
A prouder heart than Luke's. When Isabel
Had to her house returned, the old Man said,
'He shall depart to-morrow'. To this word
The Housewife answered, talking much of things
Which, if at such short notice he should go, 320
Would surely be forgotten. But at length
She gave consent, and Michael was at ease.

    Near the tumultuous brook of Greenhead Ghyll,
In that deep valley, Michael had designed
To build a Sheep-fold; and, before he heard 325
The tidings of his melancholy loss,
For this same purpose he had gathered up
A heap of stones, which by the streamlet's edge
Lay thrown together, ready for the work.
With Luke that evening thitherward he walked: 330
And soon as they had reached the place he stopped,
And thus the old Man spake to him:—'My Son,
To-morrow thou wilt leave me: with full heart
I look upon thee, for thou art the same

77

That wert a promise to me ere thy birth,   335
And all thy life hast been my daily joy.
I will relate to thee some little part
Of our two histories; 'twill do thee good
When thou art from me, even if I should touch
On things thou canst not know of.——After thou   340
First cam'st into the world—as oft befalls
To new-born infants—thou didst sleep away
Two days, and blessings from thy Father's tongue
Then fell upon thee. Day by day passed on,
And still I loved thee with increasing love.   345
Never to living ear came sweeter sounds
Than when I heard thee by our own fire-side
First uttering, without words, a natural tune;
While thou, a feeding babe, didst in thy joy
Sing at thy Mother's breast. Month followed month,   350
And in the open fields my life was passed
And on the mountains; else I think that thou
Hadst been brought up upon thy Father's knees.
But we were playmates, Luke: among these hills,
As well thou knowest, in us the old and young   355
Have played together, nor with me didst thou
Lack any pleasure which a boy can know'.
Luke had a manly heart; but at these words
He sobbed aloud. The old Man grasped his hand,
And said, 'Nay, do not take it so—I see   360
That these are things of which I need not speak.
—Even to the utmost I have been to thee
A kind and a good Father: and herein
I but repay a gift which I myself
Received at others' hands; for, though now old   365
Beyond the common life of man, I still
Remember them who loved me in my youth.
Both of them sleep together: here they lived,

As all their Forefathers had done; and when
At length their time was come, they were not loth   370
To give their bodies to the family mould.
I wished that thou should'st live the life they lived:
But, 'tis a long time to look back, my Son,
And see so little gain from threescore years.
These fields were burthened when they came to me;   375
Till I was forty years of age, not more
Than half of my inheritance was mine.
I toiled and toiled; God blessed me in my work,
And till these three weeks past the land was free.
—It looks as if it never could endure   380
Another Master. Heaven forgive me, Luke,
If I judge ill for thee, but it seems good
That thou should'st go'.
                    At this the old Man paused;
Then, pointing to the stones near which they stood,   385
Thus, after a short silence, he resumed:
'This was a work for us; and now, my Son,
It is a work for me. But, lay one stone—
Here, lay it for me, Luke, with thine own hands.
Nay, Boy, be of good hope;—we both may live   390
To see a better day. At eighty-four
I still am strong and hale;—do thou thy part;
I will do mine.—I will begin again
With many tasks that were resigned to thee:
Up to the heights, and in among the storms,   395
Will I without thee go again, and do
All works which I was wont to do alone,
Before I knew thy face.—Heaven bless thee, Boy!
Thy heart these two weeks has been beating fast
With many hopes; it should be so—yes—yes—   400
I knew that thou could'st never have a wish
To leave me, Luke: thou hast been bound to me

Only by links of love: when thou art gone,
What will be left to us!—But, I forget
My purposes. Lay now the corner-stone,   405
As I requested; and hereafter, Luke,
When thou art gone away, should evil men
Be thy companions, think of me, my Son,
And of this moment; hither turn thy thoughts,
And God will strengthen thee: amid all fear   410
And all temptation, Luke, I pray that thou
May'st bear in mind the life thy Fathers lived,
Who, being innocent, did for that cause
Bestir them in good deeds. Now, fare thee well—
When thou return'st, thou in this place wilt see   415
A work which is not here: a covenant
'Twill be between us; but, whatever fate
Befall thee, I shall love thee to the last,
And bear thy memory with me to the grave'.

   The Shepherd ended here; and Luke stooped down,   420
And, as his Father had requested, laid
The first stone of the Sheep-fold. At the sight
The old Man's grief broke from him; to his heart
He pressed his Son, he kissèd him and wept;
And to the house together they returned.   425
—Hushed was that House in peace, or seeming peace,
Ere the night fell:—with morrow's dawn the Boy
Began his journey, and when he had reached
The public way, he put on a bold face;
And all the neighbours, as he passed their doors,   430
Came forth with wishes and with farewell prayers,
That followed him till he was out of sight.

   A good report did from their Kinsman come,
Of Luke and his well-doing: and the boy
Wrote loving letters, full of wondrous news,   435
Which, as the Housewife phrased it, were throughout

'The prettiest letters that were ever seen'.
Both parents read them with rejoicing hearts.
So, many months passed on: and once again
The Shepherd went about his daily work   440
With confident and cheerful thoughts; and now
Sometimes when he could find a leisure hour
He to that valley took his way, and there
Wrought at the Sheep-fold. Meantime Luke began
To slacken in his duty; and, at length,   445
He in the dissolute city gave himself
To evil courses: ignominy and shame
Fell on him, so that he was driven at last
To seek a hiding-place beyond the seas.

    There is a comfort in the strength of love;   450
'Twill make a thing endurable, which else
Would overset the brain, or break the heart:
I have conversed with more than one who well
Remember the old Man, and what he was
Years after he had heard this heavy news.   455
His bodily frame had been from youth to age
Of an unusual strength. Among the rocks
He went, and still looked up to sun and cloud,
And listened to the wind; and, as before,
Performed all kinds of labour for his sheep,   460
And for the land, his small inheritance.
And to that hollow dell from time to time
Did he repair to build the Fold of which
His flock had need. 'Tis not forgotten yet
The pity which was then in every heart   465
For the Old Man—and 'tis believed by all
That many and many a day he thither went,
And never lifted up a single stone.

    There, by the Sheep-fold, sometimes was he seen
Sitting alone, or with his faithful Dog,   470

Then old, beside him, lying at his feet.
The length of full seven years, from time to time,
He at the building of this Sheep-fold wrought,
And left the work unfinished when he died.
Three years, or little more, did Isabel   475
Survive her Husband: at her death the estate
Was sold, and went into a stranger's hand.
The Cottage which was named the EVENING STAR
Is gone—the ploughshare has been through the ground
On which it stood; great changes have been wrought   480
In all the neighbourhood:—yet the oak is left
That grew beside their door; and the remains
Of the unfinished Sheep-fold may be seen
Beside the boisterous brook of Greenhead Ghyll.

To A Young Lady

Who had been reproached for taking long walks in the country

Dear Child of Nature, let them rail!
—There is a nest in a green dale,
A harbour and a hold;
Where thou, a Wife and Friend, shalt see
Thy own heart-stirring days, and be   5
A light to young and old.

There, healthy as a shepherd boy,
And treading among flowers of joy
Which at no season fade,
Thou, while thy babes around thee cling,   10
Shalt show us how divine a thing
A Woman may be made.

Thy thoughts and feelings shall not die,
Nor leave thee, when grey hairs are nigh,
A melancholy slave;   15
But an old age serene and bright,
And lovely as a Lapland night,
Shall lead thee to thy grave.

Written in March

The Cock is crowing,
The stream is flowing,
The small birds twitter,
The lake doth glitter,
The green field sleeps in the sun;   5
The oldest and youngest
Are at work with the strongest;
The cattle are grazing,
Their heads never raising;
There are forty feeding like one!   10

Like an army defeated
The snow hath retreated,
And now doth fare ill
On the top of the bare hill;
The Ploughboy is whooping—anon—anon: 15
There's joy in the mountains;
There's life in the fountains;
Small clouds are sailing,
Blue sky prevailing;
The rain is over and gone!

83

To the Cuckoo

O blithe New-comer! I have heard,
I hear thee and rejoice.
O Cuckoo! shall I call thee Bird,
Or but a wandering Voice?

While I am lying on the grass   5
Thy twofold shout I hear;
From hill to hill it seems to pass
At once far off, and near.

Though babbling only to the Vale,
Of sunshine and of flowers,   10
Thou bringest unto me a tale
Of visionary hours.

Thrice welcome, darling of the Spring!
Even yet thou art to me
No bird, but an invisible thing,   15
A voice, a mystery;

The same whom in my schoolboy days
I listened to; that Cry
Which made me look a thousand ways
In bush, and tree, and sky.   20

To seek thee did I often rove
Through woods and on the green;
And thou wert still a hope, a love;
Still longed for, never seen.

And I can listen to thee yet; 25
Can lie upon the plain
And listen, till I do beget
That golden time again.

O blessèd Bird! the earth we pace
Again appears to be 30
An unsubstantial, faery place;
That is fit home for Thee!

The Rainbow

My heart leaps up when I behold
    A rainbow in the sky:
So was it when my life began;
So is it now I am a man;
So be it when I shall grow old, 5
    Or let me die!
The Child is father of the Man;
And I could wish my days to be
Bound each to each by natural piety.

Resolution and Independence

I

There was a roaring in the wind all night;
The rain came heavily and fell in floods;
But now the sun is rising calm and bright;
The birds are singing in the distant woods;
Over his own sweet voice the Stock-dove broods; 5
The Jay makes answer as the Magpie chatters;
And all the air is filled with pleasant noise of waters.

II

All things that love the sun are out of doors;
The sky rejoices in the morning's birth;
The grass is bright with rain-drops;—on the moors   10
The hare is running races in her mirth;
And with her feet she from the plashy earth
Raises a mist; that, glittering in the sun,
Runs with her all the way, wherever she doth run.

III

I was a Traveller then upon the moor;   15
I saw the hare that raced about with joy;
I heard the woods and distant waters roar;
Or heard them not, as happy as a boy:
The pleasant season did my heart employ:
My old remembrances went from me wholly;   20
And all the ways of men, so vain and melancholy.

IV

But, as it sometimes chanceth, from the might
Of joy in minds that can no further go,
As high as we have mounted in delight
In our dejection do we sink as low;   25
To me that morning did it happen so;
And fears and fancies thick upon me came;
Dim sadness—and blind thoughts, I knew not, nor could name.

V

I heard the sky-lark warbling in the sky;
And I bethought me of the playful hare: 30
Even such a happy Child of earth am I;
Even as these blissful creatures do I fare;
Far from the world I walk, and from all care;

But there may come another day to me—
Solitude, pain of heart, distress, and poverty.   35

VI

My whole life I have lived in pleasant thought
As if life's business were a summer mood;
As if all needful things would come unsought
To genial faith, still rich in genial good;
But how can He expect that others should   40
Build for him, sow for him, and at his call
Love him, who for himself will take no heed at all

VII

I thought of Chatterton, the marvellous Boy,
The sleepless Soul that perished in his pride;
Of Him who walked in glory and in joy   45
Following his plough, along the mountain-side:
By our own spirits are we deified:
We Poets in our youth begin in gladness;
But thereof come in the end despondency and madness.

VIII

Now, whether it were by peculiar grace   50
A leading from above, a something given,
Yet it befell that, in this lonely place,
When I with these untoward thoughts had striven,
Beside a pool bare to the eye of heaven
I saw a Man before me unawares: 55
The oldest man he seemed that ever wore grey hairs.

IX

As a huge stone is sometimes seen to lie
Couched on the bald top of an eminence;

Wonder to all who do the same espy,
By what means it could thither come, and whence;   60
So that it seems a thing endued with sense:
Like a sea-beast crawled forth, that on a shelf
Of rock or sand reposeth, there to sun itself;

X

Such seemed this Man, not all alive nor dead,
Nor all asleep—in his extreme old age: 65
His body was bent double, feet and head
Coming together in life's pilgrimage;
As if some dire constraint of pain, or rage
Of sickness felt by him in times long past,
A more than human weight upon his frame had cast.   70

XI

Himself he propped, limbs, body, and pale face,
Upon a long grey staff of shaven wood:
And, still as I drew near with gentle pace,
Upon the margin of that moorish flood
Motionless as a cloud the old Man stood,   75
That heareth not the loud winds when they call;
And moveth all together, if it move at all.

XII

At length, himself unsettling, he the pond
Stirred with his staff, and fixedly did look
Upon the muddy water, which he conned,   80
As if he had been reading in a book:
And now a stranger's privilege I took;
And, drawing to his side, to him did say,
'This morning gives us promise of a glorious day'.

XIII

A gentle answer did the old Man make,   85
In courteous speech which forth he slowly drew;
And him with further words I thus bespake,
'What occupation do you there pursue?
This is a lonesome place for one like you'.
Ere he replied, a flash of mild surprise   90
Broke from the sable orbs of his yet-vivid eyes.

XIV

His words came feebly, from a feeble chest,
But each in solemn order followed each,
With something of a lofty utterance drest—
Choice word and measured phrase, above the reach   95
Of ordinary men; a stately speech;
Such as grave Livers do in Scotland use,
Religious men, who give to God and man their dues.

XV

He told, that to these waters he had come
To gather leeches, being old and poor: 100
Employment hazardous and wearisome!
And he had many hardships to endure:
From pond to pond he roamed, from moor to moor;
Housing, with God's good help, by choice or chance;
And in this way he gained an honest maintenance.   105

XVI

The old Man still stood talking by my side;
But now his voice to me was like a stream
Scarce heard; nor word from word could I divide;
And the whole body of the Man did seem
Like one whom I had met with in a dream;   110

Or like a man from some far region sent,
To give me human strength, by apt admonishment.

XVII

My former thoughts returned: the fear that kills
And hope that is unwilling to be fed;
Cold, pain, and labour, and all fleshly ills;   115
And mighty Poets in their misery dead.
—Perplexed, and longing to be comforted,
My question eagerly did I renew,
'How is it that you live, and what is it you do?'

XVIII

He with a smile did then his words repeat;   120
And said that, gathering leeches, far and wide
He travelled; stirring thus about his feet
The waters of the pools where they abide.
'Once I could meet with them on every side;
But they have dwindled long by slow decay;   125
Yet still I persevere, and find them where I may'.

XIX

While he was talking thus, the lonely place,
The old Man's shape, and speech—all troubled me:
In my mind's eye I seemed to see him pace
About the weary moors continually,   130
Wandering about alone and silently.
While I these thoughts within myself pursued,
He, having made a pause, the same discourse renewed.

XX

And soon with this he other matter blended,
Cheerfully uttered, with demeanour kind,   135

But stately in the main; and, when he ended,
I could have laughed myself to scorn to find
In that decrepit Man so firm a mind.
'God,' said I, 'be my help and stay secure;
I'll think of the Leech-gatherer on the lonely moor!'   140

Composed upon Westminster Bridge

September 3, 1802

Earth has not anything to show more fair:
Dull would he be of soul who could pass by
A sight so touching in its majesty:
This City now doth, like a garment, wear
The beauty of the morning; silent, bare,   5
Ships, towers, domes, theatres, and temples lie
Open unto the fields, and to the sky;
All bright and glittering in the smokeless air.
Never did sun more beautifully steep
In his first splendour, valley, rock, or hill;   10
Ne'er saw I, never felt, a calm so deep!
The river glideth at his own sweet will:
Dear God! the very houses seem asleep;
And all that mighty heart is lying still!

'It is a Beauteous Evening'

It is a beauteous evening, calm and free,
The holy time is quiet as a Nun
Breathless with adoration; the broad sun
Is sinking down in its tranquillity;

The gentleness of heaven broods o'er the Sea: 5
Listen! the mighty Being is awake,
And doth with his eternal motion make
A sound like thunder—everlastingly.
Dear Child! dear Girl! that walkest with me here,
If thou appear untouched by solemn thought, 10
Thy nature is not therefore less divine:
Thou liest in Abraham's bosom all the year;
And worshipp'st at the Temple's inner shrine,
God being with thee when we know it not.

Composed near Calais on the Road leading to Ardres

August 7, 1802

Jones! as from Calais southward you and I
Went pacing side by side, this public Way
Streamed with the pomp of a toc-credulous day,
When faith was pledged to new-born Liberty:
A homeless sound of joy was in the sky: 5
From hour to hour the antiquated Earth
Beat like the heart of Man: songs, garlands, mirth,
Banners, and happy faces, far and nigh!
And now, sole register that these things were,
Two solitary greetings have I heard, 10
'*Good morrow, Citizen!*' a hollow word,
As if a dead man spake it! Yet despair
Touches me not, though pensive as a bird
Whose vernal coverts winter hath laid bare.

To Toussaint L'Ouverture

Toussaint, the most unhappy man of men!
Whether the whistling Rustic tend his plough
Within thy hearing, or thy head be now
Pillowed in some deep dungeon's earless den;—
O miserable Chieftain! where and when   5
Wilt thou find patience! Yet die not; do thou
Wear rather in thy bonds a cheerful brow:
Though fallen thyself, never to rise again,
Live, and take comfort. Thou hast left behind
Powers that will work for thee; air, earth, and skies;   10
There's not a breathing of the common wind
That will forget thee; thou hast great allies;
Thy friends are exultations, agonies,
And love, and man's unconquerable mind.

On Milton

Milton! thou shouldst be living at this hour:
England hath need of thee: she is a fen
Of stagnant waters: altar, sword, and pen,
Fireside, the heroic wealth of hall and bower,
Have forfeited their ancient English dower   5
Of inward happiness. We are selfish men,
Oh! raise us up, return to us again;
And give us manners, virtue, freedom, power.
Thy soul was like a Star, and dwelt apart;
Thou hadst a voice whose sound was like the sea: 10

Pure as the naked heavens, majestic, free,
So didst thou travel on life's common way,
In cheerful godliness; and yet thy heart
The lowliest duties on herself did lay.

O Friend! I know not which way I must look

O Friend! I know not which way I must look
For comfort, being, as I am, opprest,
To think that now our life is only drest
For show; mean handy-work of craftsman, cook,
Or groom!—We must run glittering like a brook   5
In the open sunshine, or we are unblest:
The wealthiest man among us is the best:
No grandeur now in nature or in book
Delights us. Rapine, avarice, expense,
This is idolatry; and these we adore: 10
Plain living and high thinking are no more:
The homely beauty of the good old cause
Is gone; our peace, our fearful innocence,
And pure religion breathing household laws.

The World is too much with us

The world is too much with us; late and soon,
Getting and spending, we lay waste our powers:
Little we see in Nature that is ours;
We have given our hearts away, a sordid boon!
This Sea that bares her bosom to the moon;   5

The winds that will be howling at all hours,
And are up-gathered now like sleeping flowers:
For this, for everything, we are out of tune;
It moves us not.—Great God! I'd rather be
A Pagan suckled in a creed outworn;   10
So might I, standing on this pleasant lea,
Have glimpses that would make me less forlorn;
Have sight of Proteus rising from the sea;
Or hear old Triton blow his wreathèd horn.

The Solitary Reaper

Behold her, single in the field,
Yon solitary Highland Lass!
Reaping and singing by herself;
Stop here, or gently pass!
Alone she cuts and binds the grain,   5
And sings a melancholy strain;
O listen! for the Vale profound
Is overflowing with the sound.

No Nightingale did ever chaunt
More welcome notes to weary bands   10
Of travellers in some shady haunt,
Among Arabian sands:
A voice so thrilling ne'er was heard
In spring-time from the Cuckoo-bird,
Breaking the silence of the seas   15
Among the farthest Hebrides.

Will no one tell me what she sings?—
Perhaps the plaintive numbers flow

For old, unhappy, far-off things,
And battles long ago: 20
Or is it some more humble lay,
Familiar matter of to-day?
Some natural sorrow, loss, or pain,
That has been, and may be again?

Whate'er the theme, the Maiden sang   25
As if her song could have no ending;
I saw her singing at her work,
And o'er the sickle bending;—
I listened, motionless and still;
And, as I mounted up the hill,   30
The music in my heart I bore,
Long after it was heard no more.

Stepping Westward

While my Fellow-traveller and I were walking by the side of Loch
Ketterine, one fine evening after sunset, in our road to a Hut where,
in the course of our Tour, we had been hospitably entertained some
weeks before, we met, in one of the loneliest parts of that solitary region,
two well-dressed Women, one of whom said to us, by way of greeting,
'What, you are stepping westward?'

'*What, you are stepping westward!*'—'*Yea.*'
—'Twould be a *wildish* destiny,
If we, who thus together roam
In a strange Land, and far from home,
Were in this place the guests of Chance: 5
Yet who would stop, or fear to advance,
Though home or shelter he had none,
With such a sky to lead him on?

The dewy ground was dark and cold;
Behind, all gloomy to behold;   10
And stepping westward seemed to be
A kind of *heavenly* destiny:
I liked the greeting; 'twas a sound
Of something without place or bound;
And seemed to give me spiritual right   15
To travel through that region bright.

The voice was soft, and she who spake
Was walking by her native lake:
The salutation had to me
The very sound of courtesy: 20
Its power was felt; and while my eye
Was fixed upon the glowing Sky,
The echo of the voice enwrought
A human sweetness with the thought
Of travelling through the world that lay   25
Before me in my endless way.

The Affliction of Margaret

I

Where art thou, my beloved Son,
Where art thou, worse to me than dead?
Oh find me, prosperous or undone!
Or, if the grave be now thy bed,
Why am I ignorant of the same   5
That I may rest; and neither blame
Nor sorrow may attend thy name?

II

Seven years, alas! to have received
No tidings of an only child;
To have despaired, have hoped, believed,   10
And been for evermore beguiled;
Sometimes with thoughts of very bliss!
I catch at them, and then I miss;
Was ever darkness like to this?

III

He was among the prime in worth,   15
An object beauteous to behold;
Well born, well bred; I sent him forth
Ingenuous, innocent, and bold:
If things ensued that wanted grace,
As hath been said, they were not base;   20
And never blush was on my face.

IV

Ah! little doth the young-one dream,
When full of play and childish cares,
What power is in his wildest scream,
Heard by his mother unawares!   25
He knows it not, he cannot guess:
Years to a mother bring distress;
But do not make her love the less.

V

Neglect me! no, I suffered long,
From that ill thought; and, being blind,   30
Said, 'Pride shall help me in my wrong:
Kind mother have I been, as kind
As ever breathed:' and that is true;
I've wet my path with tears like dew,
Weeping for him when no one knew.   35

VI

My Son, if thou be humbled, poor,
Hopeless of honour and of gain,
Oh! do not dread thy mother's door;
Think not of me with grief and pain:
I now can see with better eyes;   40
And worldly grandeur I despise,
And fortune with her gifts and lies.

VII

Alas! the fowls of heaven have wings,
And blasts of heaven will aid their flight;
They mount—how short a voyage brings   45
The wanderers back to their delight!
Chains tie us down by land and sea;
And wishes, vain as mine, may be
All that is left to comfort thee.

VIII

Perhaps some dungeon hears thee groan,   50
Maimed, mangled by inhuman men;
Or thou upon a desert thrown
Inheritest the lion's den;
Or hast been summoned to the deep,
Thou, thou and all thy mates, to keep   55
An incommunicable sleep.

IX

I look for ghosts; but none will force
Their way to me: 'tis falsely said
That there was ever intercourse
Between the living and the dead;   60
For, surely, then I should have sight
Of him I wait for day and night,
With love and longings infinite.

My apprehensions come in crowds;
I dread the rustling of the grass;   65
The very shadows of the clouds
Have power to shake me as they pass:
I question things and do not find
One that will answer to my mind;
And all the world appears unkind.   70

XI
Beyond participation lie
My troubles, and beyond relief:
If any chance to heave a sigh,
They pity me, and not my grief.
Then come to me, my Son, or send   75
Some tidings that my woes may end;
I have no other earthly friend!

From *Elegiac Stanzas*

Suggested by a picture of Peele Castle, in a storm,
painted by Sir George Beaumont

I was thy neighbour once, thou rugged Pile!
Four summer weeks I dwelt in sight of thee:
I saw thee every day; and all the while
Thy Form was sleeping on a glassy sea.

So pure the sky, so quiet was the air!   5
So like, so very like, was day to day!
Whene'er I looked, thy Image still was there;
It trembled, but it never passed away.

How perfect was the calm! it seemed no sleep;
No mood, which season takes away, or brings: 10
I could have fancied that the mighty Deep
Was even the gentlest of all gentle Things.

Ah! THEN, if mine had been the Painter's hand,
To express what then I saw; and add the gleam,
The light that never was, on sea or land,   15
The consecration, and the Poet's dream;

I would have planted thee, thou hoary Pile
Amid a world how different from this!
Beside a sea that could not cease to smile;
On tranquil land, beneath a sky of bliss.   20

Thou shouldst have seemed a treasure-house divine
Of peaceful years; a chronicle of heaven;—
Of all the sunbeams that did ever shine
The very sweetest had to thee been given.

A Picture had it been of lasting ease,   25
Elysian quiet, without toil or strife;
No motion but the moving tide, a breeze,
Or merely silent Nature's breathing life.

Such, in the fond illusion of my heart,
Such Picture would I at that time have made: 30
And seen the soul of truth in every part,
A steadfast peace that might not be betrayed.

So once it would have been,—'tis so no more;
I have submitted to a new control:
A power is gone, which nothing can restore;   35
A deep distress hath humanized my soul.

She was a Phantom of Delight

She was a Phantom of delight
When first she gleamed upon my sight;
A lovely Apparition, sent
To be a moment's ornament;
Her eyes as stars of Twilight fair;   5
Like Twilight's, too, her dusky hair:
But all things else about her drawn
From May-time and the cheerful Dawn;
A dancing shape, an Image gay,
To haunt, to startle, and way-lay.   10

I saw her upon nearer view,
A Spirit, yet a Woman too!
Her household motions light and free,
And steps of virgin-liberty;
A countenance in which did meet   15
Sweet records, promises as sweet;
A Creature not too bright or good
For human nature's daily food;
For transient sorrows, simple wiles,
Praise, blame, love, kisses, tears, and smiles.   20

And now I see with eye serene
The very pulse of the machine;
A Being breathing thoughtful breath,
A Traveller between life and death;
The reason firm, the temperate will,   25
Endurance, foresight, strength, and skill;

A perfect Woman, nobly planned,
To warn, to comfort, and command;
And yet a Spirit still, and bright
With something of angelic light.

Ode

On Intimations of Immortality from Recollections of Early Childhood

The Child is father of the Man;
And I could wish my days to be
Bound each to each by natural piety.

I

There was a time when meadow, grove, and stream,
The earth, and every common sight,
To me did seem
Apparelled in celestial light,
The glory and the freshness of a dream.   5
It is not now as it hath been of yore;—
Turn wheresoe'er I may,
By night or day,
The things which I have seen I now can see no more.

II

The Rainbow comes and goes,   10
And lovely is the Rose,
The Moon doth with delight
Look round her when the heavens are bare,
Waters on a starry night
Are beautiful and fair;   15
The sunshine is a glorious birth;
But yet I know, where'er I go,
That there hath past away a glory from the earth.

III

Now, while the birds thus sing a joyous song,
    And while the young lambs bound   20
        As to the tabor's sound,
To me alone there came a thought of grief:
A timely utterance gave that thought relief,
        And I again am strong:
The cataracts blow their trumpets from the steep;   25
  No more shall grief of mine the season wrong;
  I hear the Echoes through the mountains throng,
The Winds come to me from the fields of sleep,
        And all the earth is gay;
           Land and sea   30
     Give themselves up to jollity,
       And with the heart of May
    Doth every Beast keep holiday;—
        Thou child of joy,
Shout round me, let me hear thy shouts, thou happy
    Shepherd-boy!   35

IV

Ye blessèd Creatures, I have heard the call
    Ye to each other make; I see
The heavens laugh with you in your jubilee;
    My heart is at your festival,
    My head hath its coronal,   40
The fulness of your bliss, I feel—I feel it all.
       Oh evil day! if I were sullen
       While Earth herself is adorning,
        This sweet May-morning,
       And the Children are culling   45
        On every side,
  In a thousand valleys far and wide,
  Fresh flowers; while the sun shines warm,
And the Babe leaps up on his Mother's arm:—

I hear, I hear, with joy I hear! 50
—But there's a Tree, of many, one,
A single Field which I have looked upon,
Both of them speak of something that is gone:
  The Pansy at my feet
  Doth the same tale repeat: 55
Whither is fled the visionary gleam?
Where is it now, the glory and the dream?

     V

Our birth is but a sleep and a forgetting:
The Soul that rises with us, our life's Star,
  Hath had elsewhere its setting, 60
  And cometh from afar:
  Not in entire forgetfulness,
  And not in utter nakedness,
But trailing clouds of glory do we come
  From God, who is our home: 65
Heaven lies about us in our infancy!
Shades of the prison-house begin to close
  Upon the growing Boy,
But He beholds the light, and whence it flows,
  He sees it in his joy; 70
The Youth, who daily farther from the east
  Must travel, still is Nature's Priest,
  And by the vision splendid
  Is on his way attended;
At length the Man perceives it die away, 75
And fade into the light of common day.

     VI

Earth fills her lap with pleasures of her own;
Yearnings she hath in her own natural kind,
And, even with something of a Mother's mind,

And no unworthy aim, 80
The homely Nurse doth all she can
To make her Foster-child, her Inmate Man,
Forget the glories he hath known,
And that imperial palace whence he came.

VII

Behold the Child among his new-born blisses, 85
A six years' Darling of a pigmy size!
See, where 'mid work of his own hand he lies,
Fretted by sallies of his mother's kisses,
With light upon him from his father's eyes!
See, at his feet, some little plan or chart, 90
Some fragment from his dream of human life,
Shaped by himself with newly-learned art;
A wedding or a festival,
A mourning or a funeral;
And this hath now his heart, 95
And unto this he frames his song:
Then will he fit his tongue
To dialogues of business, love, or strife:
But it will not be long
Ere this be thrown aside, 100
And with new joy and pride
The little Actor cons another part;
Filling from time to time his 'humorous stage'
With all the Persons, down to palsied Age,
That life brings with her in her equipage; 105
As if his whole vocation
Were endless imitation.

VIII

Thou, whose exterior semblance doth belie
Thy Soul's immensity;

Thou best Philosopher who yet dost keep   110
Thy heritage, thou Eye among the blind,
That, deaf and silent, read'st the eternal deep,
Haunted for ever by the eternal mind,—
      Mighty Prophet! Seer blest!
      On whom those truths do rest,   115
Which we are toiling all our lives to find,
In darkness lost, the darkness of the grave;
Thou, over whom thy Immortality
Broods like the Day, a Master o'er a Slave,
A presence which is not to be put by;   120
      To whom the grave
Is but a lonely bed without the sense or sight
      Of day or the warm light,
A place of thought where we in waiting lie;
Thou little Child, yet glorious in the might   125
Of heaven-born freedom on thy being's height,
Why with such earnest pains dost thou provoke
The years to bring the inevitable yoke,
Thus blindly with thy blessedness at strife?
Full soon thy Soul shall have her earthly freight,   130
And custom lie upon thee with a weight,
Heavy as frost, and deep almost as life!

IX
      O joy! that in our embers
      Is something that doth live,
      That nature yet remembers   135
      What was so fugitive!
The thought of our past years in me doth breed
Perpetual benediction: not indeed
For that which is most worthy to be blest;
Delight and liberty, the simple creed   140
Of Childhood, whether busy or at rest,

With new-fledged hope still fluttering in his breast:—
  Not for these I raise
     The song of thanks and praise;
  But for those obstinate questionings   145
  Of sense and outward things,
  Fallings from us, vanishings;
  Blank misgivings of a Creature
Moving about in worlds not realized,
High instincts before which our mortal Nature   150
Did tremble like a guilty Thing surprised:
    But for those first affections,
    Those shadowy recollections,
      Which, be they what they may,
Are yet the fountain-light of all our day,   155
Are yet a master-light of all our seeing;
    Uphold us, cherish, and have power to make
Our noisy years seem moments in the being
    Of the eternal Silence: truths that wake,
      To perish never: 160
Which neither listlessness, nor mad endeavour,
      Nor man nor Boy,
Nor all that is at enmity with joy,
Can utterly abolish or destroy!
  Hence in a season of calm weather   165
    Though inland far we be,
Our souls have sight of that immortal sea
    Which brought us hither,
    Can in a moment travel thither,
And see the Children sport upon the shore,   170
And hear the mighty waters rolling evermore.

X

Then sing, ye Birds, sing, sing a joyous song!
And let the young Lambs bound

As to the tabor's sound!
We in thought will join your throng,   175
  Ye that pipe and ye that play,
  Ye that through your hearts to-day
  Feel the gladness of the May!
What though the radiance which was once so bright
Be now for ever taken from my sight,   180
  Though nothing can bring back the hour
Of splendour in the grass, of glory in the flower;
  We will grieve not, rather find
  Strength in what remains behind;
  In the primal sympathy   185
  Which having been must ever be;
  In the soothing thoughts that spring
  Out of human suffering;
  In the faith that looks through death,
In years that bring the philosophic mind.   190

XI

And O, ye Fountains, Meadows, Hills, and Groves,
Forebode not any severing of our loves!
Yet in my heart of hearts I feel your might;
I only have relinquished one delight
To live beneath your more habitual sway.   195
I love the Brooks which down their channels fret,
Even more than when I tripped lightly as they;
The innocent brightness of a new-born Day
  Is lovely yet;
The Clouds that gather round the setting sun   200
Do take a sober colouring from an eye
That hath kept watch o'er man's mortality;
Another race hath been, and other palms are won.
Thanks to the human heart by which we live,
Thanks to its tenderness, its joys, and fears,   205

To me the meanest flower that blows can give
Thoughts that do often lie too deep for tears.

At the Grave of Burns, 1803

Seven Years after his Death

I shiver, Spirit fierce and bold,
At thought of what I now behold:
As vapours breathed from dungeons cold
    Strike pleasure dead,
So sadness comes from out the mould   5
    Where Burns is laid.

And have I then thy bones so near,
And thou forbidden to appear?
As if it were thyself that's here,
    I shrink with pain;   10
And both my wishes and my fear
    Alike are vain.

Off weight—nor press on weight! away
Dark thoughts!—they came, but not to stay;
With chastened feelings would I pay   15
    The tribute due
To him, and aught that hides his clay
    From mortal view.

Fresh as the flower whose modest worth
He sang, his genius 'glinted' forth,   20
Rose like a star that touching earth,
    For so it seems,
Doth glorify its humble birth
    With matchless beams.

The piercing eye, the thoughtful brow,   25
The struggling heart, where be they now?—
Full soon the Aspirant of the plough,
        The prompt, the brave,
Slept, with the obscurest, in the low
        And silent grave.   30

I mourned with thousands, but as one
More deeply grieved, for He was gone
Whose light I hailed when first it shone,
        And showed my youth
How Verse may build a princely throne   35
        On humble truth.

Alas! where'er the current tends,
Regret pursues and with it blends,—
Huge Criffel's hoary top ascends
        By Skiddaw seen,—   40
Neighbours we were, and loving friends
        We might have been;

True friends though diversely inclined;
But heart with heart and mind with mind,
Where the main fibres are entwined,   45
        Through Nature's skill,
May even by contraries be joined
        More closely still.

The tear will start, and let it flow;
Thou 'poor Inhabitant below,'   50
At this dread moment—even so—
        Might we together
Have sate and talked where gowans blow,
        Or on wild heather.

What treasures would have then been placed   55
Within my reach; of knowledge graced
By fancy what a rich repast!
      But why go on?—
Oh! spare to sweep, thou mournful blast,
      His grave grass-grown.   60

There, too, a Son, his joy and pride,
(Not three weeks past the Stripling died,)
Lies gathered to his Father's side,
      Soul-moving sight!
Yet one to which is not denied   65
      Some sad delight.

For *he* is safe, a quiet bed
Hath early found among the dead,
Harboured where none can be misled,
      Wronged, or distrest;   70
And surely here it may be said
      That such are blest.

And oh for Thee, by pitying grace
Checked oft-times in a devious race,
May He, who halloweth the place   75
      Where Man is laid,
Receive thy Spirit in the embrace
      For which it prayed!

Sighing I turned away; but ere
Night fell I heard, or seemed to hear,   80
Music that sorrow comes not near,
      A ritual hymn,
Chanted in love that casts out fear
      By Seraphim.

From *The White Doe of Rylstone*

The only voice which you can hear
Is the river murmuring near.
—When soft!—the dusky trees between,
And down the path through the open green,
Where is no living thing to be seen;   5
And through yon gateway, where is found,
Beneath the arch with ivy bound,
Free entrance to the church-yard ground—
Comes gliding in with lovely gleam,
Comes gliding in serene and slow,   10
Soft and silent as a dream,
A solitary Doe!
White she is as lily of June,
And beauteous as the silver moon
When out of sight the clouds are driven   15
And she is left alone in heaven;
Or like a ship some gentle day
In sunshine sailing far away,
A glittering ship, that hath the plain
Of ocean for her own domain.   20

Lie silent in your graves, ye dead!
Lie quiet in your church-yard bed!
Ye living, tend your holy cares;
Ye multitude, pursue your prayers;
And blame not me if my heart and sight   25
Are occupied with one delight!
'Tis a work for sabbath hours
If I with this bright Creature go:
Whether she be of forest bowers,

From the bowers of earth below;   30
Or a Spirit for one day given,
A pledge of grace from purest heaven.

   What harmonious pensive changes
Wait upon her as she ranges
Round and through this Pile of state   35
Overthrown and desolate!
Now a step or two her way
Leads through space of open day,
Where the enamoured sunny light
Brightens her that was so bright;   40
Now doth a delicate shadow fall,
Falls upon her like a breath,
From some lofty arch or wall,
As she passes underneath:
Now some gloomy nook partakes   45
Of the glory that she makes,—
High-ribbed vault of stone, or cell,
With perfect cunning framed as well
Of stone, and ivy, and the spread
Of the elder's bushy head;   50
Some jealous and forbidding cell,
That doth the living stars repel,
And where no flower hath leave to dwell.

   The presence of this wandering Doe
Fills many a damp obscure recess   55
With lustre of a saintly show;
And, reappearing, she no less
Sheds on the flowers that round her blow
A more than sunny liveliness.
But say, among these holy places,   60
Which thus assiduously she paces,

Comes she with a votary's task,
Rite to perform, or boon to ask?
Fair Pilgrim! harbours she a sense
Of sorrow, or of reverence? 65
Can she be grieved for quire or shrine,
Crushed as if by wrath divine?
For what survives of house where God
Was worshipped, or where Man abode;
For old magnificence undone; 70
Or for the gentler work begun
By Nature, softening and concealing,
And busy with a hand of healing?
Mourns she for lordly chamber's hearth
That to the sapling ash gives birth; 75
For dormitory's length laid bare
Where the wild rose blossoms fair;
Or altar, whence the cross was rent,
Now rich with mossy ornament?
—She sees a warrior carved in stone, 80
Among the thick weeds, stretched alone;
A warrior, with his shield of pride
Cleaving humbly to his side,
And hands in resignation prest,
Palm to palm, on his tranquil breast; 85
As little she regards the sight
As a common creature might:
If she be doomed to inward care,
Or service, it must lie elsewhere,
—But hers are eyes serenely bright, 90
And on she moves—with pace how light!
Nor spares to stoop her head, and taste
The dewy turf with flowers bestrown,
And thus she fares, until at last
Beside the ridge of a grassy grave 95

In quietness she lays her down;
Gentle as a weary wave
Sinks, when the summer breeze hath died,
Against an anchored vessel's side;
Even so, without distress, doth she   100
Lie down in peace, and lovingly.

Sonnet

Mark the concentred hazels that enclose
Yon old grey Stone, protected from the ray
Of noontide suns:—and even the beams that play
And glance, while wantonly the rough wind blows,
Are seldom free to touch the moss that grows   5
Upon that roof, amid embowering gloom,
The very image framing of a Tomb,
In which some ancient Chieftain finds repose
Among the lonely mountains.—Live, ye trees!
And thou, grey Stone, the pensive likeness keep   10
Of a dark chamber where the Mighty sleep:
For more than Fancy to the influence bends
When solitary Nature condescends
To mimic Time's forlorn humanities.

'Surprised by Joy'

Surprised by joy—impatient as the Wind
I turned to share the transport—Oh! with whom
But Thee, deep buried in the silent tomb,
That spot which no vicissitude can find?
Love, faithful love, recalled thee to my mind—
But how could I forget thee? Through what power
Even for the least division of an hour,

Have I been so beguiled as to be blind
To my most grievous loss!—That thought's return
Was the worst pang that sorrow ever bore,   10
Save one, one only, when I stood forlorn,
Knowing my heart's best treasure was no more;
That neither present time, nor years unborn
Could to my sight that heavenly face restore.

After-thought

I thought of Thee, my partner and my guide,
As being past away.—Vain sympathies!
For, backward, Duddon! as I cast my eyes,
I see what was, and is, and will abide;
Still glides the Stream, and shall for ever glide;   5
The Form remains, the Function never dies;
While we, the brave, the mighty, and the wise,
We Men, who in our morn of youth defied
The elements, must vanish;—be it so!
Enough, if something from our hands have power   10
To live, and act, and serve the future hour;
And if, as toward the silent tomb we go,
Through love, through hope, and faith's transcendent dower,
We feel that we are greater than we know.

Mutability

From low to high doth dissolution climb,
And sink from high to low, along a scale
Of awful notes, whose concord shall not fail;
A musical but melancholy chime,
Which they can hear who meddle not with crime,   5
Nor avarice, nor over-anxious care.

Truth fails not; but her outward forms that bear
The longest date do melt like frosty rime,
That in the morning whitened hill and plain
And is no more; drop like the tower sublime   10
Of yesterday, which royally did wear
His crown of weeds, but could not even sustain
Some casual shout that broke the silent air,
Or the unimaginable touch of Time.

Processions

Suggested on a Sabbath Morning in the Vale of Chamouny

To appease the Gods; or public thanks to yield;
Or to solicit knowledge of events,
Which in her breast Futurity concealed;
And that the past might have its true intents
Feelingly told by living monuments—   5
Mankind of yore were prompted to devise
Rites such as yet Persepolis presents
Graven on her cankered walls, solemnities
That moved in long array before admiring eyes.

The Hebrews thus, carrying in joyful state   10
Thick boughs of palm, and willows from the brook,
Marched round the altar—to commemorate
How, when their course they through the desert took,
Guided by signs which ne'er the sky forsook,
They lodged in leafy tents and cabins low;   15
Green boughs were borne, while, for the blast that shook
Down to the earth the walls of Jericho,
Shouts rise, and storms of sound from lifted trumpets blow!

And thus in order, 'mid the sacred grove
Fed in the Libyan waste by gushing wells,   20
The priests and damsels of Ammonian Jove
Provoked responses with shrill canticles;
While, in a ship begirt with silver bells,
They round his altar bore the hornèd God,
Old Cham, the solar Deity, who dwells   25
Aloft, yet in a tilting vessel rode,
When universal sea the mountains overflowed.

Why speak of Roman Pomps? the haughty claims
Of Chiefs triumphant after ruthless wars;
The feast of Neptune—and the Cereal Games,   30
With images, and crowns, and empty cars;
The dancing Salii—on the shields of Mars
Smiting with fury; and a deeper dread
Scattered on all sides by the hideous jars
Of Corybantian cymbals, while the head   35
Of Cybelè was seen, sublimely turreted!

At length a Spirit more subdued and soft
Appeared—to govern Christian pageantries:
The Cross, in calm procession, borne aloft
Moved to the chant of sober litanies.   40
Even such, this day, came wafted on the breeze
From a long train—in hooded vestments fair
Enwrapt—and winding, between Alpine trees
Spiry and dark, round their House of prayer
Below the icy bed of bright ARGENTIERE.   45

Still in the vivid freshness of a dream,
The pageant haunts me as it met our eyes!
Still, with those white-robed Shapes—a living Stream,
The glacier Pillars join in solemn guise
For the same service, by mysterious ties;   50

Numbers exceeding credible account
Of number, pure and silent Votaries
Issuing or issued from a wintry fount;
The impenetrable heart of that exalted Mount.

They, too, who send so far a holy gleam   55
While they the Church engird with motion slow,
A product of that awful Mountain seem,
Poured from his vaults of everlasting snow;
Not virgin lilies marshalled in bright row,
Not swans descending with the stealthy tide,   60
A livelier sisterly resemblance show
Than the fair Forms, that in long order glide,
Bear to the glacier band—those Shapes aloft descried.

Trembling, I look upon the secret springs
Of that licentious craving in the mind   65
To act the god among external things,
To bind, on apt suggestion, or unbind;
And marvel not that antique Faith inclined
To crowd the world with metamorphosis,
Vouchsafed in pity or in wrath assigned;   70
Such insolent temptations wouldst thou miss,
Avoid these sights; nor brood o'er Fable's dark abyss!

Extempore Effusion upon the Death of James Hogg

When first descending from the moorlands,
I saw the Stream of Yarrow glide
Along a bare and open valley,
The Ettrick Shepherd was my guide.

When last along its banks I wandered,   5
Through groves that had begun to shed
Their golden leaves upon the pathways,
My steps the Border-minstrel led.

The mighty Minstrel breathes no longer,
'Mid mouldering ruins low he lies;   10
And death upon the braes of Yarrow,
Has closed the Shepherd-poet's eyes.

Nor has the rolling year twice measured,
From sign to sign, its stedfast course,
Since every mortal power of Coleridge   15
Was frozen at its marvellous source;

The rapt One, of the godlike forehead,
The heaven-eyed creature sleeps in earth:
And Lamb, the frolic and the gentle,
Has vanished from his lonely hearth.   20

Like clouds that rake the mountain-summits,
Or waves that own no curbing hand,
How fast has brother followed brother,
From sunshine to the sunless land!

Yet I, whose lids from infant slumber   25
Were earlier raised, remain to hear
A timid voice, that asks in whispers,
'Who next will drop and disappear?'

Our haughty life is crowned with darkness,
Like London with its own black wreath,   30
On which with thee, O Crabbe! forth-looking,
I gazed from Hampstead's breezy heath.

As if but yesterday departed,
Thou too art gone before; but why,
O'er ripe fruit, seasonably gathered,   35
Should frail survivors heave a sigh?

Mourn rather for that holy Spirit,
Sweet as the spring, as ocean deep;
For Her who, ere her summer faded,
Has sunk into a breathless sleep.   40

No more of old romantic sorrows,
For slaughtered Youth or love-lorn Maid!
With sharper grief is Yarrow smitten,
And Ettrick mourns with her their Poet dead.

Airey-force Valley

————Not a breath of air
Ruffles the bosom of this leafy glen.
From the brook's margin, wide around, the trees
Are steadfast as the rocks; the brook itself
Old as the hills that fed it from afar,   5
Doth rather deepen than disturb the calm
Where all things else are still and motionless.
And yet, even now, a little breeze, perchance
Escaped from boisterous winds that rage without,
Has entered, by the sturdy oaks unfelt,   10
But to its gentle touch how sensitive
Is the light ash! that, pendent from the brow
Of yon dim cave, in seeming silence makes
A soft eye-music of slow-waving boughs,
Powerful almost as vocal harmony   15
To stay the wanderer's steps and soothe his thoughts.

NOTES

THE PRELUDE

The extracts from *The Prelude*, Wordsworth's poem on the growth of his own mind, are in the original version finished in 1805-6 and first published by Ernest de Selincourt in 1926: it consists of about 9000 lines divided into thirteen books and takes the story of his life down to the time of his settling at Racedown in 1795. It was written almost as a personal confession to Coleridge, and when Wordsworth felt daunted by the prospect of the ambitious long poem he had undertaken on man, nature and society; he referred to it as 'the poem to Coleridge' and 'the poem on my earlier life'. The title *The Prelude* (i.e. to the unfinished longer work) was given it by Mrs. Wordsworth after his death.

Wordsworth says in a letter that it was 'a thing unprecedented in literary history that a man should talk so much about himself' (to Sir George Beaumont, May 1st, 1805). Like Rousseau he sets out to show to his fellow men a man in the whole truth of his nature; but the work combines the interest of vivid and veracious autobiography with that of the last epic poem in the line of Spenser and Milton: the classical dignity and sweep of the long poem is brought to an essentially modern subject, the mystery of human self-consciousness and its relation to artistic creation.

I. FAIR SEED-TIME

308. *beloved Vale:* the Vale of Esthwaite, at the north-west end of which Hawkshead is situated, where Wordsworth was at school.
329-32. These lines reflect the primitive, almost pagan attitude of Wordsworth's boyhood. He thought of nature not as the manifestation of one spirit but of several, as if a local deity inhabited every tree and mountain peak (cf. *Nutting*).
373 ff. The incident of the stolen boat took place on Ullswater.
468-9. 'When very many are skating together the sounds and noises

give an impulse to the icy trees, and the woods all round the lake *tinkle*' (Coleridge to his wife, January 14th, 1799, *Collected Letters of Samuel Taylor Coleridge*, ed. E. L. Griggs, i. 462).

7. POETIC DEDICATION

The Prelude was originally intended to consist of five books and to culminate in this episode when, in the view of the poet as he wrote, he had had as a youth a dim sense of his poetic vocation. Then in 1804 Wordsworth expanded the poem so as to include an account of his revolutionary experiences and subsequent despair and recovery.

The incident took place in his first long vacation from Cambridge. He was returning from a dance at a neighbouring farm to Hawkshead where he was staying with his old 'dame', Ann Tyson, with whom he had boarded during his schooldays.

335. *grain-tinctured:* cf. Milton, 'sky-tinctured grain' (*Paradise Lost*, v. 285). 'Grain' is used to mean a fast dye and is often associated with crimson by Chaucer and Spenser. With the literary associations in mind Wordsworth is describing the crimson of the dawn.

340. *dear Friend:* Coleridge, to whom the poem was addressed.

8. 'THERE WAS A BOY'

These lines were written in Germany in October–December 1798 and sent immediately to Coleridge who said, 'had I met these lines running wild in the deserts of Arabia, I should instantly have screamed out "Wordsworth" '. The original draft was in the first person: Wordsworth himself was the boy.

9. THE NATURE OF POETRY

Frequently in *The Prelude* Wordsworth attacks pedantic and over-intellectual schemes of education, which were coming into fashion in his day, the age of the child prodigy. Here in contrast he defends the value of sensational literature and old wives' tales as food for the imagination.

10. VISIONARY POWER

Little is said about literature in *The Prelude*, but here in the fifth book Wordsworth declares emphatically that the same power which stirs the mind to love external nature is also moved by the verbal imagination, 'the great Nature that exists in works of mighty Poets'.

11. CROSSING THE ALPS

In July 1790 Wordsworth crossed the Alps on foot during his tour through France and Italy with his lifelong friend Robert Jones. In a letter to Dorothy written in the following September and in his poem *Descriptive Sketches* (1793) he gives less remarkable accounts of his feelings of awe on this occasion. As often in his work the experience had to wait until recollection at a later period for the emotion to be rekindled and given adequate poetic expression.

Wordsworth describes his mood of ecstasy as a blend of sense perception and something beyond the world of the senses:

> when the light of sense
> Goes out in flashes that have shewn to us
> The invisible world.

His perception of the scene plays an initial part, but then the ordinary apparatus of sensation appears to be suspended; hence the ambiguity of the language. Cf. William Empson, ' "Sense" in *The Prelude*', *The Structure of Complex Words* (1951), pp. 289–305.

There is a similar description of ecstasy in *Tintern Abbey*, 41–6.

The second part of the extract, lines 553–72, was probably written in 1799 and first published in 1845.

566. *the unfettered clouds and region of the Heavens:* there are many Shakespearian echoes in *The Prelude*. This use of 'region' may recall 'the region clouds' (*Sonnet* xxxiii) and other passages.

13. LONDON IMAGES

Wordsworth spent a period of some months in London between January 1791, when he took his degree at Cambridge, and the following November when he left for France. His precise movements at this time are uncertain: as he says, 'I pitched my vagrant tent'. His vignettes of London life in Book VII are important for two reasons: they prove that the spectacle of urban humanity could stimulate his imaginative faculty as well as the scenery of the mountains; and they anticipate the poetic treatment of the impersonal cruelty of a great metropolis by Baudelaire and T. S. Eliot—the 'unreal city' (cf. particularly 627–41, 695–706).

649-51. *the Fair Holden where Martyrs suffered:* St. Bartholomew Fair was held at Smithfield, where Protestants had been burnt under Mary, on St. Bartholomew's Day (August 24th) and the subsequent days. It was visited again by Wordsworth in the company of Charles Lamb in 1802. The passage was composed two years after this visit.

17. LOVE OF NATURE AND LOVE OF MAN

This passage is strongly Miltonic in style and reminiscent of the description of paradise in the fourth book of *Paradise Lost*. Milton mentions various exotic beauty spots of legend and dismisses them as unworthy of comparison with Eden, and Wordsworth treats his Eastern pleasure garden in the same way.

123. *Gehol's famous Gardens:* Wordsworth is drawing on a description of the Chinese Imperial gardens at Seoul in Manchuria, given by John Barrow in his *Travels in China* (1804), pp. 127-33. Like Coleridge, Wordsworth was an inveterate reader of travel books.

130-1. The 'Domes of Pleasure' recall the pleasure dome in Coleridge's *Kubla Khan.*

191. *Nor such as Spenser fabled:* cf. *Shepheardes Calender*, Maye, 9-14:

> Yougthes folke now flocken in every where,
> To gather may buskets and smelling brere:
> And home they hasten the postes to dight,
> And all the Kirk pillours eare day light,
> With Hawthorne buds, and swete Eglantine,
> And girlonds of roses and Sopps in wine.

220. *My Household Dame:* Ann Tyson, who looked after him when he was at school at Hawkshead.

221-310. The story of the shepherd's son was originally composed in October-December 1800 as an episode for *Michael.*

23. THE FRENCH REVOLUTION

First published in Coleridge's paper *The Friend* in 1809.

25. TIME REGAINED

E. de Selincourt, following Gordon Wordsworth, has identified the scene of the gibbet as the Cowdrake Quarry below the Penrith Beacon.

Here in 1766 Thomas Parker, a butcher, was murdered by Thomas Nicholson. The body was afterwards hung in chains at a spot close to the scene of the crime, and on the turf below the gibbet were cut the letters T.P.M. (Thomas Parker murdered). Thus the initials were those of the murdered man and not, as Wordsworth states, those of the murderer.

The scene of Wordsworth's wait for the horses to bring him home is less easily identified, but may be the ridge overlooking the roads to Skelwith and Oxenfell. His father died on December 30th, 1783.

317.   *With those two dear Ones:* his sister Dorothy and Mary Hutchinson

336–9.   Wordsworth suggests the fleeting and intermittent character of his vision by passages like this and by metaphors describing it in terms of gleams and flashes. E.g. 'Gleams like the flashings of a shield', 'When the light of sense Goes out in flashes' (*Prelude*, VI. 534–5, supra).

30.   PROSPECTUS TO THE RECLUSE

Probably written in 1798. When *Home at Grasmere* was written in 1800 (intended to be Book I of Part I of *The Recluse*) these lines were used to form the conclusion. In 1814 Wordsworth prefixed the lines to *The Excursion* (Part II of *The Recluse*) when it was published in that year, calling them 'a kind of *Prospectus* of the design and scope of the whole Poem'. Since then the lines have usually been referred to as the Prospectus to *The Excursion*, but the title I have chosen is more accurate.

The poem is the most sustained and lofty of Wordsworth's efforts in the grand style of blank verse; the Miltonic influence is at its strongest —like Milton he is attempting a subject not treated before in epic form, applying the verse used for external narrative to an inner, spiritual theme, but more daringly than Milton, since without the intervention of a myth.

23.   *fit audience let me find though few:* one of the numerous Miltonic echoes:

> still govern thou my Song
> Urania, and fit audience find, though few.
>   (*Paradise Lost*, vii. 30–1).

25.   *Urania:* Plato distinguishes between the heavenly Aphrodite, Aphrodite Urania, and the earthly, Aphrodite Pandemos (*Symposium*, 180 d.). Milton makes Urania the Muse of sacred poetry in his invocation to Book VII of *Paradise Lost*.

35. *Chaos:* the formless region on the confines of the universe which was there before the universe was created. Milton's Satan journeys through Chaos from Hell to reach the earth (*Paradise Lost*, Book II).

36. *Erebus :* the classical underworld or hell.

46. *Pitches her tents:* like Jehovah watching over the Israelites on their road from Egypt (Exodus xiii).

48. *Fortunate Fields:* The fabled Atlantis spoken of by Plato, a kingdom in the Atlantic.

65. *the external world is fitted to the mind:* i.e., just as man is endowed with organs which enable him to adapt himself to his environment, to perceive it, and enjoy it, so (though this is less generally known) nature is not merely dead matter but possesses an independent vitality which man can appreciate since it offers to his mind lessons and images.

84. *The human Soul of universal earth Dreaming on things to come:* Shakespeare, *Sonnet* 107.

86. *A metropolitan temple:* the language is again close to that of Milton who invokes the Third Person of the Trinity

> that dost preferr
> Before all Temples th' upright heart and pure
> (*Paradise Lost*, i. 17–18).

33. HOME AT GRASMERE

Written early in 1800 and not published until 1888. A paean of celebration at his return to the Lakes with Dorothy at the end of December 1799. Remarkable for its reasoned and unsentimental exposition of Wordsworth's preference for the life of the countryman.

105. *bield:* refuge or shelter; a Scots dialect word and therefore italicized.

39. LINES WRITTEN IN EARLY SPRING

This and the four following poems, *Expostulation and Reply*, *The Tables Turned*, *Animal Tranquillity and Decay*, and *The Thorn*, were all written in the first half of 1798 and included in *Lyrical Ballads* later in that year.

40. EXPOSTULATION AND REPLY

15. *Matthew:* 'Like the Wanderer in "The Excursion", this Schoolmaster was made up of several both of his class and of other occupations'.

But in the Advertisement to *Lyrical Ballads* Wordsworth says that this and the following poem arose 'out of conversation with a friend who was somewhat unreasonably attached to modern books of Moral Philosophy', and the friend was Hazlitt who relates in his essay *My First Acquaintance with Poets*, 'I got into a metaphysical argument with Wordsworth while Coleridge was explaining the different notes of the nightingale to his sister, in which we neither of us succeeded in making ourselves perfectly clear and intelligible'.

42. ANIMAL TRANQUILLITY AND DECAY

1798 or earlier. An offshoot from *The Old Cumberland Beggar*. Wordsworth later softened the defiant bathos of the conclusion.

43. THE THORN

One of Wordsworth's experiments 'to ascertain how far the language of conversation in the middle and lower classes of society is adapted to the purposes of poetic pleasure'. In the 1800 Preface Wordsworth says: 'The poem . . . is not supposed to be spoken in the author's own person; the character of the loquacious narrator will sufficiently show itself in the course of the story'.

52. TINTERN ABBEY

July 1798. 'No poem of mine was composed under circumstances more pleasant for me to remember than this. I began it upon leaving Tintern, after crossing the Wye, and concluded it just as I was entering Bristol in the evening, after a ramble of 4 or 5 days with my sister. Not a line of it was altered, and not any part of it written down till I reached Bristol'. (Fenwick note).

1. *Five years have passed:* Wordsworth visited Tintern in 1793, after leaving the Isle of Wight and passing over Salisbury Plain.

146. *If solitude, or grief, or fear or pain.* A melancholy prophecy: Dorothy Wordsworth's reason was clouded in her later years.

57. THE REVERIE OF POOR SUSAN

Written perhaps as early as 1797 and published in the second edition of *Lyrical Ballads* in 1800. The anapaestic metre, also used by Blake in his *Songs of Innocence*, was common in street ballads in this period, and Wordsworth may have chosen it for this reason.

58. LUCY POEMS

Written in Germany in 1798–9, except for 'I travelled among unknown men' which is later. Lucy is an ideal character, but the poet's
feelings about Peggy Hutchinson who died young in 1796 and his
solicitude about his sister may have contributed something to the poems.
Coleridge thought that 'A slumber did my spirit seal' was written to
suggest what Wordsworth would have felt at the death of his sister. See
H. M. Margoliouth, *Wordsworth and Coleridge* (1951), pp. 52–8.

58. 'STRANGE FITS OF PASSION HAVE I KNOWN'

23–4. *When down behind the cottage roof,*
        At once, the bright moon dropped.

The disappearance of the moon is seized upon by the lover as a symbol
for his own anxiety and it crystallizes his thoughts into the fear that
Lucy may be dead. The idea that natural phenomena sympathize with
human emotions, and provide as it were a field of symbolism for them,
is strong in Wordsworth. The moon, here suddenly and dramatically
extinguished, is usually connected with joy and creative life in the
poetry of the Alfoxden period (in Coleridge too, e.g. in *The Ancient
Mariner*).

61. 'SHE DWELT AMONG THE UNTRODDEN WAYS.'

2. *the springs of Dove:* Wordsworth knew a Derbyshire river of this
name, a Yorkshire one, and also a Westmorland one. But no precise
geographical reference seems to matter, or to have been intended. The
line has the effect of endowing Lucy with the gentle innocence of a
dove and the creative freshness of a mountain spring.

62. LUCY GRAY

Another Goslar poem. Founded on an actual incident, but Wordsworth departs from the facts so that instead of the child's body being
recovered there is the haunting suggestion in the last two stanzas of her
continued wandering across the moor.

64. NUTTING

Another Goslar poem. A boyhood reminiscence intended for *The
Prelude*, but afterwards 'struck out as not being wanted there'.

66. 'A WHIRL-BLAST FROM BEHIND THE HILL'

Alfoxden, spring, 1798; but not published in the *Lyrical Ballads* until 1800.

68. MICHAEL

Based on a composite treatment of recent Grasmere tradition; written between October 11th, 1800, when Wordsworth went to look at an unfinished sheep-fold pointed out at Greenhead Ghyll and December 9th when Dorothy's *Grasmere Journal* records that the poem was finished. The character of Michael was suggested by that of Thomas Poole.

82. TO A YOUNG LADY

About 1801. Published in the *Morning Post*, February 11th, 1801. The poem may have been suggested by Dorothy or by some member of the Hutchinson family, possibly Mary's sister Joanna. Out-door exercise was not quite proper for the well-bred woman in the early nineteenth century, as we learn from Jane Austen's *Pride and Prejudice*: Elizabeth Bennet excites the scorn of Darcy's friends by hurrying over to Netherfield in the mud when her sister is ill.

lovely as a Lapland night . . . : one of Wordsworth's borrowings from travel books in which he was deeply interested. The source may be Crantz: *History of Greenland*.

83. WRITTEN IN MARCH

1802. A rarity in Wordsworth's work because it deals with the pleasures of immediate, not recollected, experience. The next poem, *To the Cuckoo*, was written about the same time, and characteristically connects the song of the bird heard at present with earlier impressions: sense experience is valued for its power to evoke the 'golden time' of childhood.

85. THE RAINBOW

Composed March 26th, 1802, on the day before Wordsworth began writing the *Intimations Ode*. The mood of *The Rainbow* anticipates that of the later poem

85. RESOLUTION AND INDEPENDENCE

May–July 1802. A good example of Wordsworth's tendency, while drawing on matter of fact for his material, to edit his sources in accordance with his imaginative needs. The old leech-gatherer had been encountered two years before, but it was not on the lonely moor but on the public road near Dove Cottage; and Wordsworth was not alone but accompanied by Dorothy. She describes him in her *Grasmere Journal* as bent 'almost double' and having an interesting face; there was a rather mundane conversation about the price of leeches.

Wordsworth's 'blind thoughts' were due to worry about money; perhaps also to more complicated psychological reasons which I have discussed in the Introduction (pp. xxxiii–xxxiv).

5. *Stock-dove:* the wood-pigeon.

43. *Chatterton, the marvellous boy:* Thomas Chatterton (1752–70), Bristol boy poet who was looked back on by the romantics as a founder-hero. After for some time passing off his forgeries of medieval poems as genuine he died in poverty by his own hand in London.

45. *Him who walked:* Burns.

57 f. *As a huge stone is sometimes seen to lie:* A rock deposited by glacial action such as is frequently seen in the Lake District.

97. *in Scotland:* The original old man had been Scottish; it is interesting to note that in *The Excursion* the Wanderer was a Scot.

110. *in a Dream:* Wordsworth seems to undergo a state of trance like that experienced in the presence of sublime natural scenes (cf. *Crossing the Alps*, p. 11).

91. COMPOSED UPON WESTMINSTER BRIDGE

On the outward journey to France in the early morning of July 31st, 1802; it may have been finished on top of the coach. Dorothy writes: 'The houses were not overhung by their cloud of smoke, and they were spread out endlessly, yet the sun shone so brightly, with such a fierce light, that there was even something like the purity of one of nature's own grand spectacles.'

91. 'IT IS A BEAUTEOUS EVENING'

On the beach near Calais. August 1802. The child is Wordsworth's illegitimate daughter, Caroline, whom he met there with her mother before his approaching marriage. 'The weather was very hot. We walked by the sea shore almost every evening with Annette and Caroline. . . . It was beautiful on a calm night. . . . Caroline was delighted' (Dorothy Wordsworth, *Journal*).

92. COMPOSED NEAR CALAIS

Wordsworth refers with passionate regret to his earlier visit to

France on his pedestrian tour with his friend Robert Jones when the ideals of the Revolution were high. Now Napoleon had been proclaimed Consul for life and to Wordsworth and to many other Englishmen it seemed that the cause of liberty had been betrayed.

93.   TO TOUSSAINT L'OUVERTURE

He had liberated Haiti and been made general and governor by the French republic. When Napoleon re-established slavery he refused to obey and died in prison in 1803.

The sonnet must have been written not later than June 1802 when Toussaint was arrested and sent to Paris. It belongs to the group of sonnets on National Liberty and Independence written in the summer and autumn of this year and directed against the imperialist tyranny of Napoleon and to encourage the struggle for freedom.

93.   ON MILTON
94.   'O FRIEND, I KNOW NOT WHICH WAY I MUST LOOK'

Wordsworth's headings for these two sonnets are respectively 'London, 1802', and 'Written in London, September, 1802'. On his return to England from France, Wordsworth was dismayed by his countrymen's ill-preparedness against the ambitions of Napoleon and what seemed to him the moral decadence and irresponsibility to be found in London; he attributed this to 'the mischief engendered and fostered among us by undisturbed wealth'.

The succeeding sonnet, 'The world is too much with us', appears in a manuscript transcribed before March 1804, but its mood is so close to that of the group written in September 1802 that I am inclined to associate it with them.

95.   THE SOLITARY REAPER

Written between 1803 and 1805 and one of the poems inspired by the tour made in Scotland with Dorothy in 1803. But the immediate suggestion came from his friend Thomas Wilkinson's *Tour in Scotland* which he had read in manuscript: 'Passed by a Female who was reaping alone, she sung in Erse as she bended over her sickle, the sweetest human voice I ever heard. Her strains were tenderly melancholy, and felt delicious long after they were heard no more'.

32.   Wilkinson's line was taken over word for word.

96. STEPPING WESTWARD

Another product of the Scotch tour of 1803, but not composed, or at any rate written down, until June 1805.

'We met two neatly dressed women. One of them said to us in a friendly, soft tone of voice, "What! are you stepping westward?" I cannot describe how affecting this simple expression was in that remote place, with the western sky in front, yet glowing with the departed sun' (Dorothy Wordsworth, *Journal*).

100. ELEGIAC STANZAS

1805. Peele Castle (now spelt Piel) is in Lancashire near Barrow-in-Furness. Wordsworth's memories go back as far as 1794 when he stayed there with a cousin. Sir George Beaumont was an intimate friend of the Wordsworths. The 'deep distress' is Wordsworth's grief at the death of his brother John, lost at sea in February 1805.

15. *the light that never was:* invariably misquoted as a description of the genuine working of the imagination, whereas in the context of the poem it is applied to the pleasing but delusive fancy of the poet before a deep distress had humanized him.

102. SHE WAS A PHANTOM OF DELIGHT

Wordsworth gives 1804 as the date of composition; the poem is on his wife, Mary Hutchinson.

22. *machine:* the word is used in the eighteenth-century sense, to mean something more like the present-day 'organism'. As in a favourite book of Wordsworth, Bartram : *Travels in North and South Carolina,* 'At the return of the morning, by the powerful influence of light, the pulse of nature becomes more active, and the universal vibration of life insensibly and irresistibly moves the wondrous machine'.

103. ODE: INTIMATIONS OF IMMORTALITY FROM RECOLLECTIONS OF EARLY CHILDHOOD

When first published, in the volumes of 1807, the poem was simply called *Ode*.

Summary:

stanzas i–ii. Though nature is still lovely she does not communicate the same dream-like glory and freshness to the poet which she once did.

stanzas iii–iv. Resolved to enter into the joy of the spring he is reminded sharply by a certain tree, which he has seen before with different feelings, of the loss he has sustained; his problem is posed in the form of a question: what has become of the visionary power he once possessed?

stanza v.   The problem explained: the soul has a prior state of spiritual existence which is its proper home.

stanzas vi–viii.   The child is closer to this original state and has clearer memories of it, but they fade as the child gradually assumes by imitation the roles of adult life.

stanza ix.   Some source of consolation still remains in adult life: recollection of childhood and early life, not for its mere liberty, but for the moments of perception and intense awe and excitement which reveal in retrospect the insubstantiality of the actual world and the reality of the individual mind and of 'unknown modes of being' (cf. the incident of the boat on Ullswater described in *The Prelude*).

stanza x.   There is therefore still reason for rejoicing, though something may have been lost. Also the sense of glory has given place to an understanding of human suffering and a philosophic faith.

stanza xi.   The poet has kept faith with nature and though he has lost one rapturous kind of delight he is more habitually attuned to the pleasures of nature which for him are now always intertwined with human tenderness.

The first four stanzas propounding the question 'Whither is fled the visionary gleam?' were written in March 1802 as we learn from Dorothy's *Journal* (March 27th. 'William wrote part of an ode'). De Selincourt argues convincingly that the poem was finished before September 1804 (*Poetical Works*, Oxford edition, iv, 464–5):

'Nothing was more difficult for me in childhood than to admit the notion of death as a state applicable to a human being . . . it was not so much from feelings of animal vivacity that *my* difficulty came as from a sense of the indomitableness of the spirit within me. I used to brood over the stories of Enoch and Elijah and almost to persuade myself that, whatever might become of others, I should be translated, in something of the same way, to heaven. . . . I communed with all that I saw as something not apart from, but inherent in, my own immaterial nature. Many times while going to school have I grasped at a wall or a tree to recall myself from this abyss of idealism to the reality. At that time I was afraid of such processes. In later periods of life I have deplored a subjugation of an opposite character, and have rejoiced over the remembrances. . . .' So Wordsworth says in the note on the poem he dictated to Isabella Fenwick in his old age (1843). He goes on to defend himself from any charge of heresy which might accrue from the introduction into the poem of the idea of the soul's previous existence. Though his anxiety on the point seems fussy and unnecessary we may accept his explanation that the notion of pre-existence was adopted by him as a convenient poetic myth, sanctioned by its familiarity in classical times and especially in the doctrine of *anamnesis* or recollection set out in Plato's *Phaedo*. The doctrine helps to provide rational grounds for the experience of visionary awareness in childhood; it is not employed elsewhere in his poetry; the important thing in the poem is not the myth of pre-existence but that belief in a dimension of dimly grasped spiritual values, beyond the categories of space and time, which may be expressed either in this type of temporal metaphor, or spatially, as a heaven away from the real world.

23–4.   Professor Garrod has suggested that the 'timely utterance' was the short poem on *The Rainbow* written the day before the Ode was begun.

51.   *a Tree:* Wordsworth mentions a 'tall ash' outside his bedroom window at Colthouse which haunted him deeply in his youth.

86–90.   *A six years' Darling:* Wordsworth had particularly in mind Coleridge's son Hartley.

109–21.   Coleridge objected to this stanza as 'mental bombast or thoughts and images too great for the subject'.

147.   *Fallings from us, vanishings:* the intense idealism and failure to recognize the external world as real described in the Fenwick note. When the actual world and the 'still sad music of humanity' began to press upon the mature Wordsworth they made him feel, in his darker moments, doubtful of his identity as a person: he was then glad to remember his youthful idealism when his personal identity seemed incontrovertible and everything else subordinate to it.

110.   AT THE GRAVE OF BURNS

Wordsworth's visit took place during the Scottish tour of 1803, and the poem may have been begun then or at any rate before 1807. But it was only published in 1842 and no complete manuscript of it exists before that date, an illustration of Wordsworth's method of reserving his poetic treatment of incidents till much later. His admiration for Burns was intense; as Hölderlin says, 'He who thinks most deeply loves what is most living'.

113. THE WHITE DOE OF RYLSTONE

The White Doe of Rylstone, or the Fate of the Nortons (1815) is a narrative romance on a historical subject in the manner of Scott, the difference being that Wordsworth gives the primary interest to the inner, spiritual development of the characters. Violent action shows up by contrast the quiet devotion and non-resistance of the central character which is symbolized by the Doe.

Suggested by the old ballad *The Rising in the North*, the story tells how a Catholic family, the Nortons, join in the rebellion of the northern earls to restore the old religion (1566). But one of the eight sons, Francis, and the only sister Emily belong to the new faith, and Francis vainly attempts to dissuade them. Tragically involved, Emily sews the banner of the Cross which leads them to their death, and Francis loses his life in carrying out his father's last request to bear the banner back to the shrine of Bolton Abbey. The whole family perishes except Emily who remains with her inseparable companion the Doe to find a happiness in complete resignation.

This extract is from the opening section of the poem describing the Doe's appearance outside the Abbey after the morning service.

116. SONNET

Published in the collected poems of 1815. The date of composition is not known.

116. 'SURPRISED BY JOY—IMPATIENT AS THE WIND'

Suggested by the death of Wordsworth's daughter Catherine, which profoundly affected him, but written long afterwards.

117. AFTER-THOUGHT

The sonnet sequence *The River Duddon* to which this forms the conclusion was published in 1820 and had been composed over a number of years. Wordsworth traces the river from its source to the sea; the treatment is an interesting blend of the topographical and the symbolic, introducing general reflections on human life and growth.

117. MUTABILITY

Written in 1821 and published with the *Ecclesiastical Sonnets* in 1822.

The incident on which the poem is based occurred during a tour with Crabb Robinson and other friends in 1820. It was published in *Memorials of a Tour on the Continent* in the same year.

10-18.   *The Hebrews thus . . . :* Leviticus xxiii. 40, 42, 43.

their course . . . through the desert: the Exodus from Egypt.

21. *Ammonian Jove:* Jupiter Ammon the African deity whose shrine Alexander the Great visited, cf. Milton, *Paradise Lost*, iv. 276-7: 'Old *Cham* whom Gentiles *Ammon* call and Libyan Jove'.

27-36.   Wordsworth, a considerable reader of Roman history, is drawing on Ovid's *Fasti*, a poem on the festivals and ritual observances of ancient Rome (Book IV). The Salii, the priests of Mars, marched through the streets stamping and striking their shields. The Corybantes were the Phrygian priests of Cybele who is represented in works of art wearing a crown.

48. *those white-robed Shapes:* a monthly procession of priests and villagers carrying the Host, seen at Argentière on the Arve by Wordsworth and his fellow travellers. The white-robed figures are village women in white veils from head to foot who seem to the poet to merge into and become confused with the small pyramids of the glacier. Once again Wordsworth finds a type of the interfusion of Man and Nature.

120.   EXTEMPORE EFFUSION UPON THE DEATH OF JAMES HOGG

1835. James Hogg, poet, ballad collector, friend of Scott and author of *Private Memoirs and Confessions of a Justified Sinner,* had been known to Wordsworth. The poem was composed after reading of his death in a newspaper.

4. *the Ettrick Shepherd:* Hogg.

8. *the Border-minstrel:* Scott (died 1832).

13-16.   Coleridge died in 1834.

19-20.   Lamb died in 1834.

31.   Crabbe died in 1832.

37. *that holy Spirit:* the poetess Felicia Hemans who died in 1835.

122.   AIREY-FORCE VALLEY

A manuscript in the hand of Dora Wordsworth gives the date of this as poem September 1836. It was published in 1842.

INDEX OF TITLES AND FIRST LINES

139